# FARMHOUSE

# FARMHOUSE

Reimagining the
Classic American Icon

Editors of **Fine Homebuilding**

The Taunton Press

The Taunton Press, Inc.
63 South Main Street
Newtown, CT 06470-2344
Email: tp@taunton.com

Editor: Peter Chapman
Jacket/Cover design: Lynne Phillips
Interior design: Rita Sowins / Sowins Design
Layout: Barbara Cottingham
Front cover photo: Jeff Lendrum
Back cover photos: (top) Rob Karosis; (middle) John Gruen; (bottom) Eric Roth (ericrothphoto.com)
Half-title page photo: David Pokrivnak (pokrivnak.com), courtesy of RBF CoLab
Title page photo: Paul Finkel, courtesy of Clark Richardson Architects
Facing page photo: Benjamin Cheung, courtesy of SMOOK Architecture & Urban Design
Contents page photo: Mitch Allen, mitchallenphotography.com, courtesy of GreenSpur

Library of Congress Cataloging-in-Publication Data

Title: Farmhouse : reimagining the classic American icon / editors of Fine Homebuilding.
Other titles: Fine homebuilding.
Description: Newtown, CT : The Taunton Press, Inc., [2021] | "This book is compiled from articles that originally
    appeared in Fine Homebuilding magazine." | Summary: "The farmhouse is a classic American icon, combining
    comfort and simplicity, elegance and nostalgia, all without pretension. No matter the age or condition,
    these historic homesteads call to mind the pragmatism of the pioneers who worked the land and raised
    their families at a time when practicality was key to prosperity. But the farmhouse is more than a historic
    artifact. Farmhouse style continues to evolve into the 21st century, carrying with it the best of the past while
    adapting to our modern lifestyle. Whether built in 1720 or 2020, a farmhouse is instantly recognizable for its
    main rectangular form, gabled or lean-to additions, various outbuildings, and spartan architecture, among
    other hallmarks. While the farmhouse's use of natural materials and basic construction is indicative of its
    traditional, sensible nature, modern farmhouses might equally be built according to Passive House or other
    energy-efficient standards. Whether true to tradition or adapted for a modern lifestyle, the houses featured in
    Farmhouse are a testament to the flexibility, durability, longevity, and--above all else--the everlasting appeal of
    the American farmhouse"--
    Provided by publisher.
Identifiers: LCCN 2021021147 | ISBN 9781641551649 (hardback)
Subjects: LCSH: Farmhouses--United States--Designs and plans.
Classification: LCC NA8208.5 .F37 2021 | DDC 728/.6--dc23
LC record available at https://lccn.loc.gov/2021021147

Printed in the United States of America
10 9 8 7 6 5 4 3 2 1

This book is compiled from articles that originally appeared in *Fine Homebuilding* magazine. Unless otherwise
noted, construction costs listed were current at the time the articles first appeared.

SPECIAL THANKS TO THE AUTHORS, EDITORS, ART DIRECTORS, COPY EDITORS,
and other staff members of *Fine Homebuilding* who contributed to the development of the articles in this book.

# CONTENTS

# HALLMARKS OF THE FARMHOUSE STYLE

Understand the hall-marks of this informal style, whether you're designing a new home or remodeling a classic

BY MICHAEL MAINES

THE AMERICAN FARMHOUSE STYLE COMBINES, comfort, elegance, and nostalgia, all without pretension. It is practical and hardworking. Pared down to the essentials, the farmhouse style is flexible enough to be adapted to a variety of family types and homeowner lifestyles.

New, traditionally styled farmhouses tend to reflect homes built between 1820 and 1920, when farming was an inherent part of life for many families. Earlier, Georgian-era homes—typified by the New England Colonial and Federal styles and southern plantation homes—can also be farmhouses. Because the farmhouse is not specific to an era, the style lends itself well to modern interpretation.

Though regionally the term *farmhouse* brings different images to mind, there are many common details found on most farmhouses. Because farmhouses don't have the strict design guidelines of other, more formal architectural styles, any of these elements may not appear—but here's a look at what you can expect to find on a typical farmhouse, or should consider when designing your own project.

## SHAPED OVER TIME

Even today, a farmhouse is ideally built in a rural location or a suburban area with a rural feel—or a long view. That's not to say that the farmhouse style is not comfortable in a village or urban setting, but for the full effect it should appear to be on what was once, if not currently, a farm. Even when the surrounding area has been developed, a farmhouse can retain its presence. A vegetable garden or other casual gardens with flowers and herbs sprinkled around the property can help cultivate the farmstead feel, though an overly stylized garden may look out of place in what is meant to be a hardworking setting. A pair of marriage trees in front of the house or an orchard in back create a sense of purpose, such as providing fruit, fenceposts, or support for a rope swing.

A farmhouse always starts with a basic rectangular form, often between 20 ft. by 30 ft. and 30 ft. by 44 ft. The roof is generally a simple gable. The one exception is the popular L-shaped plan, which features a projecting cross gable. But even on these homes, one of the volumes is usually dominant. Resecting portions of the main volume, which became popular in high-style architecture beginning in the Victorian era, was too frivolous for most historic farmhouses. Modern farmhouses often play with this detail, carving out a bit of the basic box to create a more dynamic form.

As needs changed over time, gabled or lean-to additions were added to the traditional farmhouse. The biggest box was not always the first shape;

## THE TRADITIONAL FARMHOUSE

Classic farmhouses can be found throughout the country. These two projects are excellent examples of new homes that have a traditional style. The simple shapes and exterior details reflect a farmer's practical attitude, while the porches emphasize a direct relationship with the landscape. The interiors are durable and hardworking.

ABOVE: Most farmhouses begin with a basic rectangular shape. A gable roof and porches are common. Here, an entry porch provides shelter and a place to remove muddy boots. A screened porch is intended for relaxing in the shade at the end of the day. The materials used on the exterior are low maintenance, including wood lap siding, metal roofing, and metal-clad double-hung windows.

TOP: The kitchen sink is strategically located for views of farm activity. The countertop in this kitchen is highly durable recycled glass.

RIGHT: Farm kitchens are typically large and welcoming, with plenty of space in which to work. This one has a workhorse of an island instead of a traditional farm table. The cabinets are made of local maple, a Vermont tradition.

a smaller building may have served as a starting point, with a larger addition built when resources allowed. New farmhouses can be designed to easily incorporate additions, or may even be built with the appearance of additions right from the start.

In New England, we have a tradition of connecting the main house to the barn through a series of supporting buildings, known as the "big house, little house, back house, barn" layout, named after a popular book on historic farmsteads. These days, homeowners tend to have garages for their iron horses, rather than barns for animals and fodder, but the organizing principles remain the same.

In keeping with the farmstead value of resourcefulness, this four-season porch is finished with reclaimed flooring and beams. The hearth and large farm table are hallmarks of a farmhouse interior.

Nestled among mature trees with views across a soy field, this farmhouse has found the perfect setting. The rebuilt home is all Midwest vernacular, including its reproduction beveled shiplap siding and steep gable dormer.

The life of a farmer is tied closely to the land, so it makes sense to have a close connection between indoors and out. Farmhouses often connect to the outdoors through a long, narrow porch, which sometimes wraps around a corner or two, known as a farmer's porch. Porches are a flexible indoor-outdoor space. Though they may be the first thing people think of when they hear "farmhouse," plenty of farmhouses don't have this feature, or have a porch that's been closed in to add interior living space. Porches are also not necessarily on the front side of the house—they can be on the side or back as well. Traditionally, porch ceilings are painted light blue to discourage visits from birds, bugs, and evil spirits, and floor boards often run in the short direction, pitched away from the house for drainage.

Most farms and farmhouses also have one or more outbuildings, dominated by the ubiquitous yet variable barn. Sometimes the barn is positioned near the house to create a working courtyard. On traditional farms, there may also be a chicken coop, a corn crib, one or more workshop outbuildings, and various sheds for storing materials, supplies, and firewood. Modern conveniences have rendered most of these outbuildings unnecessary, but to me it doesn't feel like a farmhouse without some supporting buildings scattered around the landscape.

## PRACTICAL MATTERS

Farmers are practical by necessity, and do not use flashy or unnecessarily costly materials. They tend to stay put for generations, so it makes sense for them to invest in details that save money over the long term. Therefore, farmhouse materials are low maintenance and natural, often sourced locally if not from the building site itself. Natural stone, brick, and wood are commonly used on farmhouse exteriors. Farmhouse siding and trim tends to be simple and traditional. Clapboards installed 4 in. to the weather are typical in New England, but farmhouses around the country also feature shingles, vertical boards with or without battens, stone, brick, and stucco. Trim may be simple or elaborate, though rarely dressed up to the extent you would expect on a high-style city house.

Farmhouse roofs are pitched steeply enough to shed precipitation, usually with overhangs at the eaves and rakes. In some regions and for cost savings, rake overhangs may be omitted, and some modern farmhouses omit roof overhangs com-

## THE TRANSITIONAL FARMHOUSE

Built in all corners of the country for centuries, farmhouses can be a blend of traditional and modern styles and so are a natural fit for a transitional approach to design. By staying true to the farmer's ethos of simplicity and practicality, the new farmhouses shown here balance traditional form with materials and details that reflect contemporary materials and lifestyles.

ABOVE: This farmhouse is tall and proud, similar in style to a house just down the road. The gable roof, symmetrical window arrangement, and front porch are characteristics of Midwestern farmhouses from the early 1900s, but the porch columns are made of galvanized steel instead of wood.

LEFT: The kitchen is designed with generous windows so the cook never need wonder who is coming up the drive or what weather is rolling in from the west. Hutchlike built-ins anchor the corners, and the traditional farm table is replaced by a functioning island. Exposed timbers and industrial-steel light fixtures are inspired by the unadorned rural barn aesthetic.

pletely. Steel roofing of various types is popular for function and aesthetics on today's farmhouses. Wood shakes or shingles, natural slate, or clay tile may all be used, but asphalt shingles affordably imitate most of these materials and are much more common.

Before the late 1700s, many farmhouse exteriors weren't painted at all, or were painted only in muddy earth tones. Starting in the 1820s during the Greek Revival, off-white and light grays and tans imitating marble became popular; as the Victorian era progressed, earth tones in a wide range of mix-and-match shades gained prominence. The stark, chalky white of the titanium dioxide pigment we

have today has only been available for the last 100 years, but has become a classic farmhouse look.

Windows are usually spaced uniformly across a farmhouse facade, but are sometimes combined in groups—for example, at a bay window or picture window. As a rule, they are simple, vertically oriented rectangles. Multipane windows in various patterns and proportions are common, but modern farmhouses often omit the muntins altogether; since the only purpose they serve today is aesthetic, il fits the practical farmhouse ethos to eliminate them. Windows are usually limited to just a few different sizes, though modern farmhouses often play with the scale while keeping the proportions of traditional windows.

ABOVE: Mixing traditional and modern features allows this kitchen to feel timeless and fresh. The home-office nook reflects modern life, while the informality of a kitchen table in lieu of an island and the refrigerator tucked around the corner give the new farmhouse kitchen an old-time feel.

RIGHT: A wraparound porch takes advantage of different light and temperature conditions throughout the day and the seasons. This porch is detailed to allow unobstructed views. The metal posts and beams are a modern upgrade that set off the warm wood color of the decking and ceiling.

## WARM AND HARDWORKING INTERIORS

Unpretentious and welcoming, farmhouse interiors have a sense of warmth and openness, with inspiration drawn from traditional details and natural materials. Historically, the front rooms in the house are the more formal, public spaces, and the back is more utilitarian, but in today's floor plans these rules are often broken.

Though the way we cook has changed dramatically over the last three centuries, farmhouse kitchens may still reflect some elements of their old-time counterparts. They usually include a place to eat, whether it be an island, peninsula, or small table—sometimes, the kitchen wraps around a large worktable. There may be a fancy dining table used on special occasions, but the everyday table should be a workhorse, as useful for breaking down an animal carcass as for dining.

Some details you might expect to find in a farmhouse kitchen include painted cabinets with a mix of paneled or glass doors, open shelving, and plenty of drawers. Sometimes simple Z-back doors are used, but this occurs more often in a pantry than a kitchen. Plate and pot racks keep everyday items on display and within reach. The cabinets have face frames, ideally with inset doors and drawer fronts, and may have a furniture-like appearance. Durable stone, wood, tile, or metal countertops; glazed apron-front sinks or sinks with an integral drainboard; a range with the presence of a wood- or coal-fired cooking stove; and vintage-style, decorative lighting all have a place in today's farmhouse

## THE MODERN FARMHOUSE

As seen in these two new homes, the essentials of modern architecture—including symmetry, clean lines, and ingenious details—are in keeping with the farmhouse spirit. Wood, stone, and metal are materials commonly used to create both modern and farmhouse styles, and even reused materials —part of farmstead culture—have a place in modern design.

**ABOVE:** This new home is a great example of how setting and form establish the farmhouse style. A simple rectangular main volume, a cross gable "addition," consistent window arrangements, lap siding, and an outbuilding keep the farmstead tradition in an otherwise supermodern home.

**LEFT:** A hearth at the heart of the gathering space and simple, utilitarian bookshelves are true to the traditional farmhouse interior, even with this home's modern interior design and decor.

kitchens. Nothing is wasted on a well-run farm, so repurposed or somewhat worn items fit right into the farmhouse aesthetic. A generous but simple pantry is useful and appropriate. (For more on farmhouse kitchens, see pp. 156–173.)

There should be enough windows in the farmhouse to make the space light and bright, with available views of the farmstead. A true farmhouse also has a mudroom of some sort—an informal side or garage entry with heavy-duty surfaces and room to store outerwear and other essential items. Cubbies, a freestanding or built-in bench, and durable wood wainscoting on the walls all fit the farmhouse look.

Historically, many farmhouses had plastered walls and ceilings—but spaces were also often left unfinished in anticipation of renovations made regularly over time, so surfaces of all types are appropriate. Exposed beams and grooved boards on ceilings, simple wood wainscoting on walls, and painted or natural wood floors are all common— the more worn in, the better. Colors range from all white to rich, bright, or cool earth tones. Distressed wood, galvanized or pewter-finished metal, and classic lantern-style lighting are all appropriate touches. Modern farmhouses don't necessarily need to use period fixtures, though; farmers of old would have used the most practical fixtures available. Farmhouse doors are usually paneled, though the number and orientation of panels varies. Sliding barn doors are not historically accurate, but

RIGHT: A salvaged window sash is repurposed in the staircase to soften the look of the hardworking wall of bookshelves. In the kitchen beyond, an industrial-style pendant light reflects both the minimalistic modern and utilitarian farmhouse aesthetics.

BELOW: With open shelves, furniture-like cabinetry, and a casual kitchen table, the high-style urban interior design remains informal and functional.

This modern home stays true to the farmhouse style through the use of natural materials, including wood lap siding, a natural-stone masonry chimney, and architectural steel elements. Connected to the garage by a breezeway, the home creates the effect of an original main house with a series of additions.

they pull a practical farm detail into the home in a whimsical manner.

Some old farmhouses still have an attached privy, but virtually all have upgraded to an indoor bathroom. Décor can vary, but a claw-foot tub and pedestal or console sink always look at home in a farmhouse. Painted wood or simple tile wainscoting on the walls, a furniture-like medicine cabinet or a simple wall-hung mirror, and vintage-looking light fixtures all work well. Bathroom floors may be painted planks, classic glazed or slate tile, or something more contemporary, like natural linoleum sheet flooring.

As you've seen here, farmhouses have been designed for centuries in all corners of the country. While one can be quite different than the next, each share traits that reflect the philosophy of American farmers—simplicity and practicality of form, resourcefulness and durability of materials and construction, and a strong work ethic. It is perhaps these characteristics, more than any particular architectural details, that define the farmhouse style.

# Part 1

# FARMHOUSES

# FOUR-PART FARMHOUSE

## Uncommon design goals inform the organization of this multi-volume home

BY CLAY SMOOK

I'VE BEEN DESIGNING HOUSES AND COMMERCIAL buildings for 38 years. My projects run the gamut from custom homes to master plans for mixed-use communities, which means I bring to my residential work the perspective of an urban designer. For this house—a 2,800-sq.-ft. new build in Needham, Mass.—I wanted to not only meet the clients' goals but also make a positive impact on the neighborhood. The narrow half-acre lot is located at a three-way intersection on a busy street in a densely populated area, making it highly visible. The feedback the clients have received from nearby residents tells me that secondary goal was met.

There were a number of ways in which this project was unusual. First, the homeowners actually live in the house next door; their plan is to eventually downsize and move into this house, which was designed for single-floor living to accommodate the clients' mother, who occupies the house now, as well as their own needs when the time comes. Second, among their top priorities were the dining room and the garage—I've never had a client emphasize those functions; they usually take a back seat. I decided to design a four-volume structure inspired by historian Thomas Hubka's "big house, little house, back house, barn" idea. Described in his book of the same title, it is a type of connected farm building most commonly found in northern New England (see the sidebar on p. 17). This configuration made the best use of the site and allowed generous square footage for the dining room and the garage.

### CHARACTERIZING THE VOLUMES

The idea was to keep the forms simple, while playing with scale and proportion for architectural interest. The largest structure is meant to look like the original "big house" to which the other buildings were later added. I wanted each structure to feel autonomous, but they are linked together with structural components that I call "interstitial connectors." For example, there's an 8-ft.-wide cube between the two-story main house and the garage; the roof of it acts like a cricket between the two structures by T-boning into the otherwise independent garage roof.

I went with standing-seam metal roofs on both the dining room and the garage—as opposed to the main house, which has asphalt shingles. The metal makes those structures more striking and also supports the idea of buildings added on to the original house.

CONTINUOUS ARCHITECTURE. The design concept for this house was inspired by the evolution of old New England farmhouses, which were often added on to over time to form one sprawling structure. Here, the "big house, little house, back house, barn" idea takes the form of a main house, dining room, sleeping quarters, and garage.

## CONNECTED YET SEPARATE

From the entry onward, the primary living spaces are loaded to one side of a main corridor. The interiors are organized for single-floor living with two guest suites upstairs. The garage and master suite were sited to form a backyard courtyard, which is integral to the success of the indoor-outdoor living experience. Each volume has exposure to daylight and views from three directions.

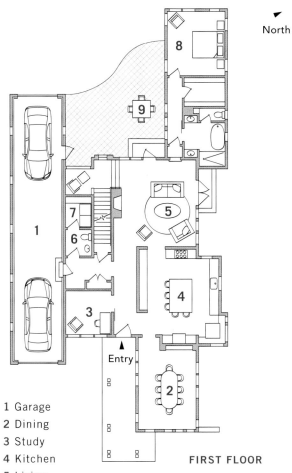

North

**FIRST FLOOR**

Entry

1 Garage
2 Dining
3 Study
4 Kitchen
5 Living
6 Powder room
7 Laundry
8 Master suite
9 Patio
10 Bedroom

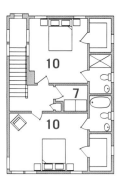

**SECOND FLOOR**

0 2 4    8 ft.

**SPECS**

**Bedrooms:** 3
**Bathrooms:** 3½
**Size:** 2,800 sq. ft.
**Location:** Needham, Mass.
**Architect:** SMOOK Architecture & Urban Design, smookarchitecture.com
**Builder:** Rockwood Custom Building, rockwoodcustombuilding.com

LEFT: FARMHOUSE STYLE. In keeping with the design concept, the no-nonsense kitchen is sized to accommodate the preparation of large family dinners. It is also arranged for aging in place.

The back of the house is meant to be just as architecturally engaging as the front—in my mind, there is no front and back. Because I am fond of courtyards, I created one by extending one of the master-bedroom walls and developing the rear elevation around it. Connecting the interiors to the outdoors is about more than putting a large sheet of glass between them. I wanted true transitional spaces, and for the clients to enjoy the feeling of being outside yet bounded by the house. When inside, they are able to look out toward views that include parts of the house, which helps to frame the landscape.

With the windows, I tried to walk the line between traditional and contemporary. Some are much larger than windows typically seen on a house of the period that inspired this one, but I prefer to use windows that are appropriate for what's happening inside. For example, in the kitchen I spec'd a sizable picture window above the built-in seating for the breakfast nook to allow natural light to fill that corner and brighten the work zone. The double-hungs tie the house to the established neighborhood, while the more modern styles give the exteriors some flair.

FRONT AND ALMOST CENTER. The dining room sits to the front of the main house, solely occupying one of the four forms. The cathedral ceiling and numerous windows create a voluminous feel in the modestly sized space.

ABOVE: ELEGANT ENTRY. The foundation was formed using a mudsill detail that has the joists slotted into, rather than on top of, the foundation, meaning the house sits low to the ground. This profile helps accentuate the front porch.

RIGHT: SLICE OF LIGHT. The double-height box bay window provides natural light and views of the rear courtyard and landscape from the second-floor guest rooms.

## SATISFYING THE PRIORITIES IN STYLE

The homeowner's mother loves hosting large Sunday dinners, so the dining room—the "little house"—was important. In fact, it is the cornerstone of the overall design and sits foremost on the lot. The exterior treatment—particularly the steeply pitched gable roof, contemporary asymmetrical window arrangement, and close proximity to the portico—was intended to draw the most attention of all the structures. The room sits atop a plinth of stone that is proud of the building—the idea was to elevate the importance of this portion of the home. Housing the room in what acts like a freestanding structure was meant to make it feel special, and the cathedral ceiling and heavy glazing create an expansive interior space. The tie to the kitchen works well functionally, but when the family is in the dining room, the work zone is out of sight, which the clients feel enhances the dining experience.

New England's covered bridges influenced the shape of the garage (or "barn"). It has a linear configuration with entrances at both ends. Most of the homes going up in the area are overwhelmed

# BIG HOUSE, LITTLE HOUSE, BACK HOUSE, BARN

Architect Thomas Hubka has written extensively about this type of connected farm building, which evolved in 19th-century northern New England as a way for farmers to organize their homesteads for mixed-farming and home-industry activities. Typically, the house and barn are joined by a series of support structures to form a continuous complex. The "big house" tends to face the road and displays the most architectural ornamentation. Formal parlors are on the first floor and bedrooms on the second. The "little house" incorporates the kitchen, and the "back house" feeds off that to form an "L." The back house connects to the barn—which houses livestock—and is used as a multipurpose workspace that might also store a bale wagon or carriage. This project is a contemporary interpretation of the building type.

**BIG HOUSE**
The kitchen, living room, and secondary bedrooms are located in the main volume.

**BACK HOUSE**
This form feeds off the main house and is given to the master suite.

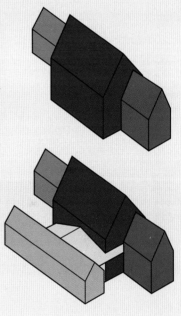

**LITTLE HOUSE**
The dining room occupies the whole of this structure, which sits to the front of the main house.

**BARN**
The garage connects to the main volume and houses up to six cars.

with garage doors, which is why I chose a tandem design to limit how much of the garage is seen from the street. There's no indication that the building is 60 ft. long; visually, it foreshortens to about half that length. The repetition of the board-and-batten panels and the trim wrap creates a balanced composition, while the small square windows call to mind the openings seen on covered bridges.

CONCENTRATED COURTYARD. The rear elevation centers around a courtyard; the backside exterior is meant to be as stimulating as the front of the house in terms of architectural interest. A mix of siding materials and window types reflects the blending of pseudo-traditional and true contemporary styles.

## A MIX OF SIDING MATERIALS

The main house is clad in 4-in. Hardie clapboards with 5/4 trim, which mimics cedar without the maintenance requirements. The rear elevation features a chimney and a double-height window with HardiePanel siding and decorative strapping. There was a time when I would have used metal to clad the chimney, but it is subject to oil-canning, so I used painted Azek to get the look of metal's crisp lines. It's a durable solution and it saves the expense of another on-site installation crew.

Because the master suite ("back house") is meant to feel like an extension of the main house, I used the same Hardie siding there. For the dining room, I spec'd 2x trim and siding from Hardie's Artisan line, which has about 7 in. of face exposure.

In addition to the covered-bridge inspiration for the garage, I considered the clients' mother's fondness for tobacco barns, which typically have vertical slats that open and close for air circulation. Covered bridges, on the other hand, often have both vertical and horizontal detailing. I wanted to

CONNECTING THE FORMS. Portions of the house are attached with "interstitial" structure intended to both demarcate and celebrate transitional spaces. Larger, more contemporary windows are used in these locations.

thread the needle between these two models. To that end, I created the look of board-and-batten siding with two patterns—one has 12 in. between battens, the other has 6 in. (I say "the look of" because it is actually Hardie sheet stock rather than individual boards.) While the garage siding adds texture, the color ties it all together. Originally, I recommended red, which would have been a literal reference to the covered bridge, but ultimately the homeowners agreed to a palette of black, gray, and white for a more 21st-century feel.

Using a mix of Boral, Azek, and Hardie board is like pattern-making. It does require the builder to make some tricky transitions between material types, and the flashing details require extra thought, but the results are exactly what we hoped for—a distinct building form that draws the eye in to look more closely.

# HOW GREAT HOUSES TAKE SHAPE

An architect explains how to use six principles of massing to shape a distinctive small home

BY JEREMIAH ECK

AFTER DESIGNING LOTS OF HOUSES, I'VE SEEN what can happen when I mention the term *massing* to clients. Their eyes roll back into that space where jargon goes to die. As pretentious as the term sounds, it nevertheless describes a fundamental design element that can't be ignored.

Massing describes the way a farmhouse (or any other type of house) looks in three dimensions: height, length, and width. The interrelationships created by these dimensions give a house its mass and determine whether it looks right. This house, designed by my partner, Paul MacNeely, sits on the shore of a small lake west of Boston. At 1,926 sq. ft., it's modest in size, yet it projects a sense of variety and function typical of larger homes. In fact, massing is a great tool for making a small house seem more spacious.

A former professor of mine used to say, "Keep it simple, but make it complex." That's just what Paul did by balancing the six principles of massing explored here. Yes, injecting this kind of complexity makes for a house that costs more than one designed with a simpler approach. But the result can be a house that's really worth coming home to.

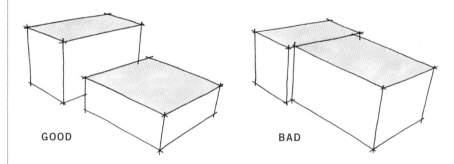

GOOD      BAD

### 1 KEEP THE SHAPES SIMPLE

A house with good massing doesn't make you wonder where to look first. The general rule is that the composition should have one dominant element. In our example, it's the taller portion of the house. Your eye goes there first, and then begins to explore the rest.

One way to make a small house seem larger is to break it into distinct parts. Start with simple, uncomplicated shapes that are easily identifiable as major or minor functions of the house. Don't overdo it; one or two major components are always better than too many. In this case, we divided the house into two wings: one for living/dining, the other for sleeping (see the floor plans on p. 22). This reflection of the inside function on the outside massing is one mark of a distinctive home.

It's also important that the separate masses of the house have strong boundaries so that they read as distinct from one another. Shadowlines from offsets and indentations achieve this goal. Note how the separation at the entry and the lower form of the one-story portion create a distinct hierarchy. The bulky alternative shown in the "bad" drawing on p. 20 stops your eye cold.

SPECS
**Bedrooms:** 3
**Bathrooms:** 2½
**Size:** 1,926 sq. ft.
**Location:** Auburn, Mass.
**Architect:** Paul MacNeely
**Builder:** Tim Cronin,
    Kinsley Homes

SCREENED PORCH

KITCHEN

ENTRY

UP

CORRIDOR

LIVING/ DINING

DECK

MASTER BEDROOM

NORTH

**FIRST FLOOR**

0  2  4    8 FT.

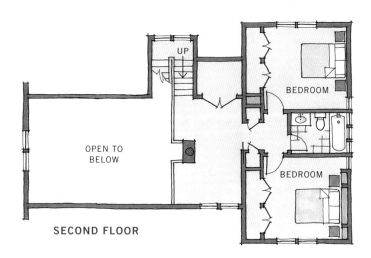

UP

OPEN TO BELOW

BEDROOM

BEDROOM

**SECOND FLOOR**

Massing is the term for how a house looks in three dimensions: height, length, and width.

A GROUP OF SHAPES. The design is just a square and a rectangle joined by a corridor that runs through the house. Yet the inset entries front and back, along with the offset corners of the house's three parts, create opportunities for each to take on a distinctive character.

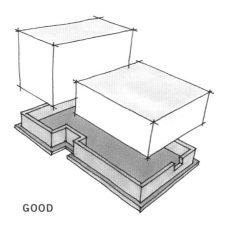

**GOOD**

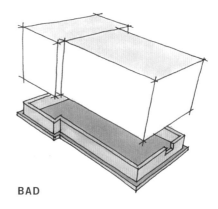

**BAD**

## 2 MAKE A STATEMENT WITH THE FOUNDATION

Realize that a small change in the foundation can make a big difference in the rest of the house. The indentations on both sides of this foundation not only begin to define the entry hall but also separate the two wings of the house.

THE ENTRY REFINED. Recessed entries provide a bit of shelter. The glass doors and generous side lites create a transparent notch between the two primary masses of the house, further distinguishing them.

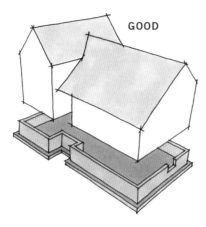

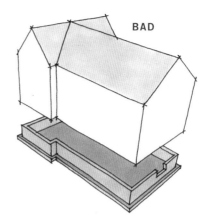

### 3 DON'T OVERDO THE ROOF

Whether a roof has a steep slope or is almost flat, with a large overhang or small, it should look at home on the house. A steep roof, for example, would be out of place on a Craftsman or ranch, house styles typified by shallow roof pitches and deep overhangs. Too many roof types can be just as confusing as too many house shapes.

This house is in New England, where steep gable roofs and their saltbox variations are ubiquitous on houses that range in style from Victorian to cottage.

The tall bedroom wing of this house presents a steep gable to the street. Although the intersecting gable over the living wing is a different pitch, there is no dissonance because the gables aren't seen side by side. Note how the intersecting ridgelines in the bad version create a static elevation. By stepping the ridgeline down, the house moves toward an assembly of distinct parts, emphasized by the triangular piece of wall on the bedroom wing over the entry.

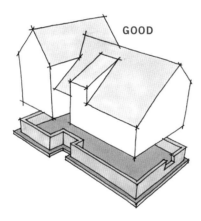

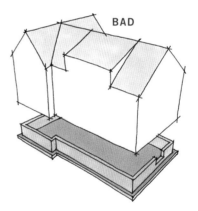

### 4 DESIGN DORMERS WITH RESTRAINT

Dormers should never overwhelm a roof by being too big, or take away from the importance of the major roof shapes by injecting incompatible forms into the composition. For the sake of consistency, we often repeat the main roof's slope in the dormer roofs. In this case, however, a simple shed roof was more appropriate for the cottage look and feel we were after. The shed dormer provides headroom

for the stair landing leading to the upstairs bedrooms, and its triangular sidewall shape echoes in scale that of the bedroom wing. Repetitive related forms such as these add complexity to a house and increase its perceived size.

The greedy dormer in the gone-wrong drawing shows what happens when a primary roof is balkanized by a bloated shed dormer.

MINOR PORTIONS REFLECT MAJOR SHAPES.
The screened porch projects from the southwest
corner of the house, topped with a hip roof that
repeats the slope of the primary roof. Three small
awning roofs with the same slope shelter the
garden shed, the door, and the band of windows.

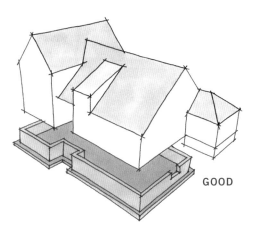

GOOD

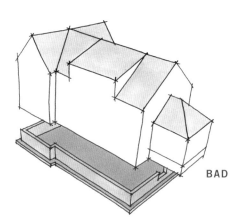

BAD

## 5 INTEGRATE ADDITIONS WITH THE MAJOR HOUSE

Additional parts of the house such as bays, porches, or even separate living components should feel like a natural outgrowth, not an afterthought, of the major house shapes. Additions are often special places, such as this home's screened porch. It is distinguished by its own roof and also embraced by the house with a portion of the main roof, where it forms a hip over the porch on the lake side. The porch is simultaneously separate from yet included in the body of the house.

When the screened porch is moved to the center of the wall rather than the corner, the connection with the main roof is lost. In addition, this central positioning of the porch in the end wall creates two hard-to-take-advantage-of walls on each side. Placing the porch at the corner makes room for big windows in the gable end, a side entry, and a little garden shed, all topped with related shed-roof awnings (photo above).

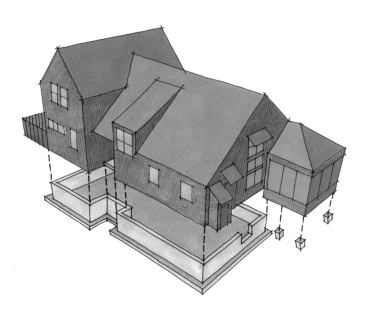

## 6 USE DETAILS WHERE THEY MAKE THE MOST IMPACT

Details are like punctuation marks. They make you pause in the right places, they emphasize important points, and they lend fluency to the message. Columns, chimneys, windows, doors, brackets, and siding materials are among the details that should enhance the look and feel of a house.

We broke this house into distinct parts to give it complexity, but we didn't stop there. For example, the largest windows are where they properly belong, in the living wing facing the lake. The smaller windows are in the bedroom wing, reinforcing the difference between the two parts.

We also changed the exterior finish on each part. The living wing is clapboard, while the bedroom wing is board-and-batten siding. The clapboards reinforce the horizontal nature of the living wing, and the board-and-batten emphasizes the vertical lines of the bedroom wing.

Finally, we used color as a unifying factor. All the material changes might have been too much, but by staining most of the exterior red, we were able to tie the various elements together. Too many colors would have been too busy and would have detracted from the overall simplicity of the house.

DETAILS EMPHASIZE THE MAJOR SHAPES. With its vertical shadowlines, board-and-batten siding gives the bedroom wing a visual lift. Horizontal clapboards on the living wing bring it down to earth. Note how the brackets supporting the roof over the deck complete the gable shape of the screened porch.

# A COLONIAL RESURRECTION

A Revolutionary War–era stone farmhouse is restored with a preservation-ist's attention to detail

BY JEFFREY DOLAN

IN THE MIDST OF THE REVOLUTIONARY WAR, farmer John Edwards erected a fieldstone house on a hill overlooking his 300-acre Pennsylvania estate. Designed in a regional variation on the Georgian style, the house's walls were constructed of stones hauled from surrounding fields and topped with a simple gable roof. In the subsequent centuries, however, neglect and misguided remodeling played havoc with the structure. By the early 2000s, the house was overgrown with vege-tation, the stonework was obscured by stucco, and the original aesthetic was compromised by ungainly renovations from the 1960s. Though unsure of what they might find beneath, our clients purchased the old farmhouse with a plan to transform it into a comfortable home in which to raise their family.

By partnering with local craftsmen who were familiar with this style, we were able to re-create the home's interior and exterior with tradi-tional details gleaned from our firm's studies of local vernacular. With all projects of this type, I find myself fascinated with the process of peeling back layers of modernization to rediscover the details and character that give homes like this their original beauty. Unlike building a new residence, where work starts with design and planning, this project by necessity began with the undoing of previous renovations to reveal clues about the original aesthetic and function of the home.

## DEMOLITION MOVES THE PROJECT FORWARD

The demolition crew stripped the interior structure down to expose thick fieldstone walls and removed several unnecessary, non-load-bearing inte-rior partitions. Water-damaged drywall, cracked and buckling plaster, and shabby carpet were removed throughout the home to reveal beautifully aged hand-hewn chestnut beams, white-oak flooring, and stone walls. We chose to feature the few original architectural details that survived— including the stonework, original beams, and flooring—and complemented them with appropriate reproductions as we added back layers of finish. For example, the original fireplace mantels of the living room had been removed and replaced with more "modern" Victorian mantels that were later painted a bright aqua sometime in the 1960s. With no visual record

DIAMOND IN THE ROUGH. Obscured by stucco for decades (inset photo), the fieldstone shell of John Edwards's 1776 homestead lends an unmistakable character to the house.

## EVOLUTION OF A FLOOR PLAN

Additions and alterations spanning four centuries make this farmhouse a unique study in how a home evolves to meet changing needs. Most visible is the addition of space, with the introduction of separate areas designed for specific functions, such as dining, cooking, bathing, and later, parking the car.

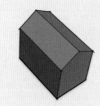

**18TH CENTURY**
Constructed of fieldstone in 1776, the original farmhouse consisted of a two-story rectangle with fireplaces on each gable end and an entrance on the long side.

**19TH CENTURY**
A two-story addition (c. 1820), also made of local stone, provided additional gathering and sleeping space for the family as the farm grew in size.

RE-CREATING THE INTERIOR. Adapting a home built more than 200 years ago to the demands of contemporary living is hard enough; doing so while faithfully restoring the original spirit of the structure requires an exceptional understanding of traditional architecture. The rehabilitated dining room retains its straightforward colonial charm.

of the original mantels, we drew on our research of colonial-era Pennsylvania farmhouses to customize a period-appropriate design crafted by McGinnis Millwork of Parkesburg, Pa. As storage wasn't part of John Edwards's master plan, we took every opportunity to develop built-in cabinetry and closets wherever we could.

The house has a single, box-winder staircase that is a hallmark of a colonial stone farmhouse. Although the staircase is small, dark, and somewhat difficult to traverse from floor to floor, modern code requirements made creating a new staircase within the confines of the existing house impractical, so we left it alone.

## 20TH CENTURY

In the 1960s, a garage was added, with a mudroom linking it to the main house. The 1776 space, serving as a living room, was divided. The 1820 addition became a kitchen and dining room.

## 21ST CENTURY

A family room was added off the kitchen, along with a new patio. The kitchen and dining room were rejoined, and the partition dividing the living room was removed. The primary entrance now leads into a spacious mudroom.

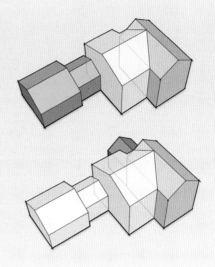

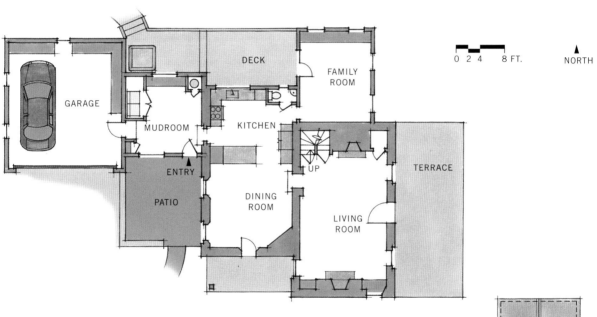

0 2 4 8 FT.

NORTH

GARAGE

DECK

FAMILY ROOM

MUDROOM

KITCHEN

ENTRY

UP

TERRACE

PATIO

DINING ROOM

LIVING ROOM

**SPECS**

**Bedrooms:** 3

**Bathrooms:** 2½

**Size:** 2,800 sq. ft.

**Cost:** $250 per sq. ft.

**Year built:** original, 1776; latest renovation, 2011

**Location:** Media, Pa.

**Architect:** Period Architecture Ltd.,

    periodarchitectureltd.com

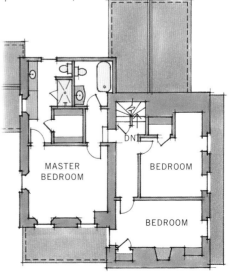

MASTER BEDROOM

DN

BEDROOM

BEDROOM

TOP: MEETING HALFWAY. Creating a comfortable home for the 21st century meant designing a roomy, updated kitchen and an equally spacious mudroom. Details such as reproduction iron hardware keep the newer spaces grounded in the colonial age.

ABOVE: HINTING AT HISTORY. A family-room addition puts comfort first but leaves a shared stone wall uncovered as a nod to the home's original structure.

CELEBRATION OF STRUCTURE. In the master bedroom, both the stone wall and the chestnut ceiling beams are revealed.

## RESTORING EXTERIOR CHARM

After stripping the stucco from the exterior, mason Cleveland Ambris began the painstaking task of repointing the entire house with a historically correct, hydraulic, lime-based (rather than portland-cement-based) mortar mix. Used for centuries, lime-based mortar is more flexible and won't crack or spall. The entire process took Ambris about three months to complete.

In need of an immediate fix to stop leaks from deteriorating the house any further, the roof was recovered with asphalt shingles. Eventually, a new cedar-shake roof will be the final step in restoring the farmhouse.

Vinyl siding at the garage and pent roof sheltering the original front door was replaced with cedar siding. The exterior of the framed mudroom extension, added in the 1960s, was disguised with a more period-appropriate veneer of chinked oak logs.

During a previous renovation, the original wood windows and antique glass had been replaced with mass-produced vinyl windows retrofitted into the masonry openings. Casings and jambs were sloppily packed in to make up any discrepancy in sizes. We selected wood replacement windows by Marvin with historically appropriate details and six-over-six divided lites. These windows enabled us to maintain the character of the home while taking advantage of their thermal performance. In addition, each window was custom-made to its specific opening for a tight fit.

In old homes, it can be challenging to incorporate modern conveniences such as heating, cooling, and plumbing. The bathrooms were renovated in their original locations to take advantage of existing plumbing lines. For heating and cooling, we installed two heat pumps: one in the basement to service the first floor and one in the attic to service the second floor. This approach eliminated the need for soffits and chases of ductwork to deliver heating and cooling from room to room and from floor to floor. Wrought-iron registers presented a great material choice appropriate for this older home.

## RESOURCES

KITCHEN AND MILLWORK
Kevin McGinnis, McGinnis Millwork,
mcginnismillwork.com

LIGHT FIXTURES AND HARDWARE
Heritage Metalworks, heritage-metalworks.com

HARDWARE
Monroe Coldren & Son, monroecoldren.com

SHUTTERS
Vixen Hill, vixenhill.com

WINDOWS
Marvin Windows & Doors, marvin.com

MASONRY
Cleveland Ambris, Ambris Residential Masonry & Restoration

PLASTER
Jack Thompson

PAINT
Authentic Colors of Philadelphia line,
Finnaren & Haley, fhpaint.com

LIVING-ROOM TABLE AND CHAIRS
McLimans Furniture Warehouse, mclimans.com

CHANDELIERS
Irvin's Country Tinware, irvins.com

## RESEARCH

NATIONAL
Library of Congress, loc.gov
National Trust for Historic Preservation,
preservationnation.org

LOCAL
Preservation Alliance for Greater Philadelphia,
preservationalliance.com
The Athenaeum of Philadelphia,
philaathenaeum.org
Colonial Pennsylvania Plantation,
colonialplantation.org

## HALLMARKS OF A STYLE

Popular in England in the 17th and 18th centuries and subsequently adopted in the colonies, the Georgian style of this house harks back to classical forms of the Italian Renaissance. In Pennsylvania, these homes typically took the form of a two-story brick or stone structure with a gable roof and a symmetrical arrangement of windows and doors on the front. While many hallmarks of the style may have originated across the ocean, materials used here were largely indigenous. Few interior details survived in the house, but its structure offered an authentic framework upon which those details could be convincingly re-created.

INTERIOR
1 Plaster on interior walls
2 Locally forged iron hardware
3 Raised panel or cope-and-pattern (vertical board) walls at fireplaces
4 Box-winder staircase
5 Plaster firebox
6 Fireplaces at end walls
7 Brick or stone hearth
8 Wood floors, casing, and baseboards

EXTERIOR
9 Stone or brick construction
10 Small roofs to protect entries
11 Window-pane ratio of 8:10 (8 in. wide by 10 in. tall)
12 Window shutters
13 Gable-roof pitch between 8-in-12 and 10-in-12
14 Stone quoins
15 Chimneys on gable end

## A FAMILY ROOM OFFERS A PLACE TO RELAX

Despite all the additions over the years, the house lacked an informal family-gathering space. To remedy this, we designed a family-room addition with a one-and-a-half-story cathedral ceiling off one side of the kitchen; on another side, we added access to a new patio for outdoor entertaining. Double French doors allow light and visual connection to the landscape, which were important to our clients.

While the furnishings here are comfortably modern, we imbued this new family room with colonial-inspired details such as character-grade oak floors, reclaimed beadboard wainscot, and a long, built-in window seat with cubbies for storage. The exterior stone wall was left exposed for its textural aesthetic and for a subtle connection between this new space and the original 1776 house.

# MODERN MASONRY FARMHOUSE

A unique home in North Carolina conjures old-world sensibilities with some surprising details

BY CHARLES MILLER

AN INCONSPICUOUS LANE, PAVED WITH YELLOW-ochre marl, winds its way through a soybean field, past rows of fledgling Cynthiana grapevines to emerge at the entry of a house called "Broken China." It's the retirement home for a longtime resident of the Washington, D.C., metropolitan area, a reclusive mathematician who grew up in the nearby farmlands here in eastern North Carolina. The house got its name when the owner's nephews, visiting the freshly plowed farm, came upon bits of pottery and broken dishware. This evidence of the farm's history slipped easily into a handle that stuck, and while its silhouette and subdued palette echo the simple farmhouses that dot the surrounding landscape, Broken China's roots extend all the way to France.

## MAKE A ROBUST, EUROPEAN-STYLE FARMHOUSE

Architect Tina Govan remembers her first discussions with the owner of Broken China. He talked about his travels in Europe, mostly France, where he has photographed and made paintings of his favorite French farmhouses. Plenty of details distinguished the houses from one another, but the common threads were clear. They all had simple gabled shapes and thick masonry walls. Each house also had an attached barn, or one nearby, and room for gardens, orchards, and a small vineyard.

Those were the broad strokes—the canvas for the sturdy details that breathed life into each house. Windowsills deep enough for a 5-gal. flowerpot, thick wood doors and shutters with diagonal bracing held fast by rivets, and stone thresholds worn down by centuries of passing boots were the sorts of honest underpinnings that gave these houses authenticity. That, and the revealed structure of rafters, posts, braces, and floor joists.

BUILDING ON A LONG TRADITION. Along the north edge of a 50-acre piece of farmland, the house is oriented on an east-west axis for maximum southern exposure. The Galvalume metal roof channels irrigation water to cisterns at opposite corners of the house. Roof-mounted photovoltaic panels are in the long-term plan. The barn at the west end is offset to allow daylight into the house and to shelter the patio from the afternoon sun.

PUTTING THE FRENCH IN THE FARMHOUSE. From the heart of Burgundy, a Lacanche range is the undeniable centerpiece of the kitchen. It's the splurge, made possible in part by its more humble surroundings: counters and cabinets by IKEA and simple wooden shelves instead of cabinets.

## THICK WALLS ENVELOP A PLAN YEARS IN THE MAKING

Govan and the owner evaluated a variety of building systems to get the thick walls right. Rammed-earth and straw-bale walls were both in contention, but they never considered a double-stud-wall approach to get the look without the mass. Says Govan, "We didn't want to fake it." They eventually settled on lightweight concrete blocks made from autoclaved aerated concrete, or AAC (see the sidebar on p. 42). A mainstay in European construction, AAC was introduced in the United States in the 1960s, but it still hasn't developed a strong following despite its many attributes and ardent supporters.

The owner's desire to return to North Carolina for his retirement was a driving factor in the project —his plans for how to live in the house have shaped its interior function as much as his European travels shaped its outward appearance.

### SPECS

**Bedrooms:** 2
**Bathrooms:** 1½
**Size:** house, 2,825 sq. ft.; barn, 700 sq. ft.
**Location:** Trenton, N.C.
**Architect:** Tina Govan, Raleigh, N.C.,
tinagovan.com
**Builder:** Scott Construction, Beaufort, N.C.

GENTLE CURVES WHERE THE WALLS CHANGE THICKNESS. The first-floor walls are 24 in. thick: two rows of 12-in. blocks side by side. The second-floor walls are 16 in. thick: two rows of 8-in. blocks. The curved blocks shown here create a gentle transition between the two, made more seamless with two coats of plaster.

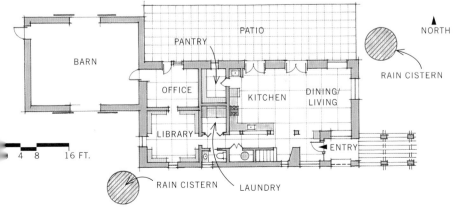

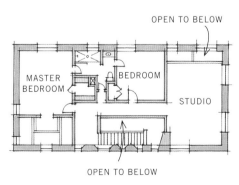

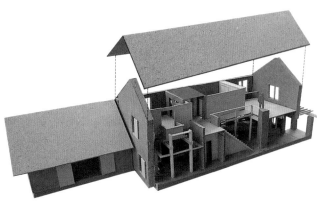

STRUCTURE AS DECOR. Just inside the front door, the ceiling opens up to reveal the parade of trusses that support the roof. Throughout the house, its parts are also the finish, assembled with a precision appropriate to trimwork (note the staggered nail pattern in the column on the left). Below, a model enables Govan to get a three-dimensional sense of how the spaces relate to one another in a house. For this one, she used ¾-in.-thick Homasote for the exterior walls.

The plan weds two offset rectangles. The larger is the two-story house; the smaller is an attached barn. The spaces within the largely open plan are tailored to support and sustain the owner's varied interests. Painting, writing, gourmet cooking, and learning to make wine are all on his retirement to-do list. A well-stocked library adjacent to the office is at the ready. In the open kitchen, a Lacanche range anchors the L-shaped workspace.

The front door is at the southeast corner of the house and is framed by a quartet of columns supporting a shady trellis that leads to a protected entry. This low-ceilinged alcove bursts into a two-story space, righting a wrong that has always frustrated Govan: "We build these beautiful, intricate structures, especially roofs, and then cover them up with various kinds of skins, such as drywall. It's a shame."

THE LOFT UPSTAIRS. Within its thick-walled shell, a neighborhood of rooms and spaces stretches out on the second floor. The studio space is in the foreground, the guest bedroom lies just beyond it, and the master suite is in the distance.

There's no covering up here. The scissor trusses that support the roof are fully exposed. They are seen partially from the ground floor through slots that let in daylight from the second-story windows. On the second floor, the trusses can be seen across the entire length of the house.

## SHUTTERS, STUCCO, AND PLASTER

Rustic shutters flanking casement windows are ubiquitous in old French farmhouses. They look just as comfortable on Broken China, and not just for effect; they may be a welcome line of defense against flying projectiles in this hurricane-prone region. The casement windows (dynamicwindows.com) are in-swinging, which allows the owner to close the upstairs shutters easily from inside.

Stuccos and plasters that have the same permeability and compressive strength as the AAC blocks are recommended finishes for the material, and they impart the hand-troweled look of a plastered French farmhouse. Two coats of stucco, mixed to match the earthy color of the driveway, finish the exterior and tie it visually to the landscape. On the inside, two coats of plaster with enough sand in it to give it some texture unify the masonry walls into a surface that resembles a soft fabric, such as flannel or chamois. The splayed window openings and the sine-curve intersections of the first- and second-floor walls showcase this sensuous touch.

## WHY ISN'T THIS NEAR-PERFECT MATERIAL MORE POPULAR?

It's called AAC, an abbreviation for autoclaved aerated concrete, and its attributes make it sound almost too good to be true. Invented by a Swedish architect in the mid-1920s, AAC is made of readily available, inert materials. AAC is rotproof, it won't burn, termites won't eat it, it has insulating properties (a little better than R-1 per in.), it can be shaped with woodworking tools, it limits sound transmission, it doesn't grow mold or mildew, and it accepts stucco and plaster without requiring any lath. It's also 80% air, so it weighs 80% less than concrete, making it much easier to lift and transport.

So why don't we see more buildings made with AAC? Kelly Finch, who has built with AAC for years, chalks it up to the inertia of the familiar. Unlike Europe, where AAC is popular and the forests were cut down long ago, North America still has plenty of trees and carpenters.

### WORKING WITH AAC
It's hard to find builders knowledgeable about AAC who are neutral about the material. Finch was the AAC subcontractor on this project. He calls AAC "the best building product in the world." He also says, "Your plumber and electrician will hate it." More about that in a minute.

Finch likes the precise dimensions of the AAC blocks and the ease with which they can be shaped. They can be cut with carbide-tipped sawblades, drill bits, and routers. Finch also likes the simplicity of the material. Unlike ICFs (insulated concrete forms), AAC has no petroleum-based foam to worry about in a fire. Finally, he likes the way AAC walls moderate the summer sun in North Carolina. By the time the day's heat makes its way through the wall, the sun is setting. Interior temperatures remain tempered through the night as the walls slowly release their heat.

### START LEVEL, STAY LEVEL
Finch says, "Working with AAC is more like working with tile than typical concrete blocks because the AAC blocks are so uniform in size. You use a notched trowel to spread a 1/8-in.-thick layer of thinset mortar between the vertical and horizontal joints. If a block is too high, use a rasp to grind it down." Given the close tolerances, it's really important that the footings be cast absolutely level. Finch points out that AAC lends itself to being shaped, so it has inherent sculptural possibilities, such as those presented where first- and second-floor walls intersect. Finch used a bandsaw to shape a gentle, ogeelike curve into a row of blocks that merge the 24-in.-thick walls of the first floor to the 16-in.-thick walls of the second floor.

One person's sculptural opportunity is another's nuisance, however. The electricians used carbide-tipped router bits to carve channels in the laid-up blocks for the flex-conduit electrical runs. This is a noisy, dust-cloud-inducing exercise in using a router on a vertical surface. It made the electricians nostalgic for stud walls and nail-biter drill bits. Finch, however, gave the material the kind of endorsement that is hard to ignore: When he built an addition to his own house, he made it out of AAC.

YOU CAN SEE ALL THE PARTS. In the library, even the low-voltage cables that power the lights over the bookcases are visible. The polished concrete floor is warmed by water from an on-demand heater under the stairs. The mosaic contains patterns from an ancient Roman villa re-created in stone tesserae.

## PUTTING THE *VIN* IN VINTAGE

For the owner, building this house was an adventure without a deadline. His goal of making wine from his own grapes is echoed in the mosaics in the library floor. The patterns re-create those found in the ruins of a Roman villa on the island of Cyprus celebrating Dionysus, the Greek god of wine.

Next to the office is the barn, with a heavily reinforced slab floor under the area marked *future wine cisterns*. The vines are in the ground and are starting to bear clusters of fat, scarlet grapes.

# FEDERAL FARMHOUSE

A Vermont architect uses the state's energy-efficiency guidelines to craft a new zero-energy home steeped in traditional character

BY R. ANDREW GARTHWAITE

DOUG AND JOAN CALLED MY VERMONT FIRM TO explain that they had purchased property with a beautiful view and a 1950s ranch that was in terrible condition. A young professional couple who enjoys outdoor activities, they planned to remove the existing house and build a new family home. They had several goals that influenced our design work as well as the construction process. At the top of the list was a traditional exterior—a Federal-style farmhouse that would fit comfortably into its country-road setting. They also sought a compact footprint and energy-efficient performance, and they knew they wanted as few petroleum products as possible used in the construction and functioning of the house. They wanted a house that would be straightforward to maintain, with an open plan for the main living space.

It seems to me that for the last several years, high-performance homes have been developing an identifiable style that leans toward the clean lines and minimal details of modern architecture. With this project, we were able to redefine what's possible when it comes to the appearance of a superefficient home. Specifically, we showed that a home built with today's best practices that meets perhaps the most important level of energy performance—net-zero energy consumption—can have authentic, period-appropriate character.

## A SUSTAINABLE FARMHOUSE WITH ROOTS IN TRADITION

The site that Doug and Joan bought could not have been a better place for a sustainable, energy-efficient house. Not only is it environmentally and economically advantageous to build on an already developed site, but the excavator even found someone to repurpose the existing house as a hunting camp.

With beautiful views to the south and east and the road to the north, we were able to set the house along an east-west axis so the south-facing roof would receive maximum solar collection but the photovoltaic panels would be hidden from almost every public view. In this way, the street-facing elevation is all traditional Vermont farmhouse. Fortunately, many of the hallmarks of traditional architecture complement sustainable and energy-efficient design. The simple shapes lend themselves to effective air-sealing and insulation details.

As long as a project's efficiency goals and the necessary details are included from the beginning, they will survive the processes of design, budgeting, and construction. In other words, sustainability and efficiency cannot be add-ons or upgrades; they must be integrated from the start. And of course, modern building materials make both style and

TRADITIONAL IN DETAIL. The Federal-style trim around the roof-lines is a hallmark of the Vermont farmhouse vernacular. Executed with a combination of common building materials and stock moldings from Brosco, these details are more attainable than ever.

efficiency much easier to achieve. For example, double-hung windows are the tradition in Vermont, but triple-glazed double-hung units are still somewhat scarce and expensive. We installed triple-pane casement units from Kohltech—which in general perform better than double-hung windows anyway—with a meeting rail that simulates the look of double-hung windows.

We also employed a broad definition of the term *sustainable*. The locally harvested lumber, trim, and wood-flooring materials; the Vermont slate tile; and the granite counters were selected not only for their character and connection to the site, but to support the local economy as well. We also considered the energy used in the construction and functioning of the house, the comfort and health of the occupants, the house's resilience to storms, and the need to create a durable home.

## HELP FROM THE STATE

We are fortunate in Vermont to have a state-mandated organization that helps designers, builders, and homeowners achieve sustainable energy solutions. Efficiency Vermont has done extensive research to learn which sustainable design strategies and systems work best in our climate. Its High Performance Homes program sets minimum insulation and maximum air-leakage levels, as well as requirements for a number of other key components.

The Efficiency Vermont staff reviewed our schematic design and specifications and confirmed that we were on track to achieve net zero. They also provided advice throughout the process on systems and construction details. Projects that meet the High Performance Home designation are entitled to rebates. In our estimation, however, the

## TRIM DETAILS

### 1 FRONT PORCH ROOF TRIM

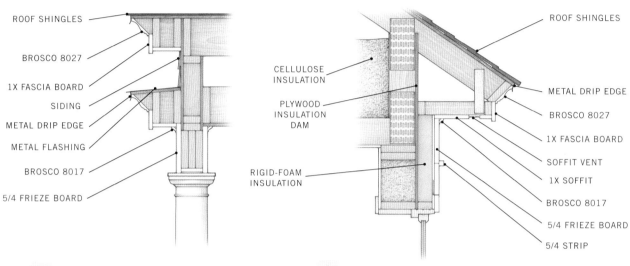

ROOF SHINGLES

BROSCO 8027

1X FASCIA BOARD

SIDING

METAL DRIP EDGE

METAL FLASHING

BROSCO 8017

5/4 FRIEZE BOARD

### 2 EAVE TRIM

ROOF SHINGLES

CELLULOSE INSULATION

PLYWOOD INSULATION DAM

RIGID-FOAM INSULATION

METAL DRIP EDGE

BROSCO 8027

1X FASCIA BOARD

SOFFIT VENT

1X SOFFIT

BROSCO 8017

5/4 FRIEZE BOARD

5/4 STRIP

### 3 GABLE EAVE EXTENSION

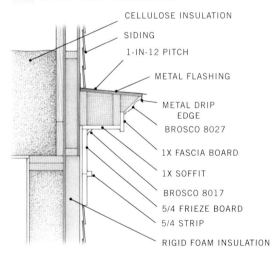

CELLULOSE INSULATION

SIDING

1-IN-12 PITCH

METAL FLASHING

METAL DRIP EDGE

BROSCO 8027

1X FASCIA BOARD

1X SOFFIT

BROSCO 8017

5/4 FRIEZE BOARD

5/4 STRIP

RIGID FOAM INSULATION

### 4 RAKE TRIM

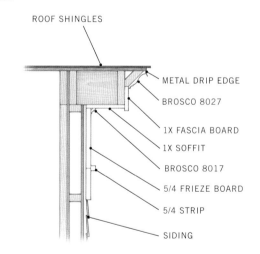

ROOF SHINGLES

METAL DRIP EDGE

BROSCO 8027

1X FASCIA BOARD

1X SOFFIT

BROSCO 8017

5/4 FRIEZE BOARD

5/4 STRIP

SIDING

---

rebates are not large enough to be a great factor when making decisions.

To heat and cool the house, we used two highly efficient electric air-source minisplit heat pumps from Mitsubishi that are rated to operate in temperatures as low as -13°F. In a radical shift from normal approaches to heating and cooling, there is no heat in the bedrooms and bathrooms. With high levels of insulation and triple-glazed windows, the interior surfaces stay warm enough to keep the radiant surface temperatures comfortable. Even on the coldest winter nights, the two small electric-resistance heaters that we installed to supplement the minisplit heat pumps rarely come on. In the end, the house is powered entirely by electricity, with a heat-pump water heater, electrical appliances, and all-LED lighting.

**ABOVE:** INTEGRATING MODERN WITH TRADITIONAL. The house's open living space is not the only break from tradition. The look of double-hung windows is implied with a faux meeting rail in these large casement windows. The deep window wells are the result of 3 in. of insulation on the outside of the walls. Still, the light fixtures and the Shaker-style cabinetry, wood flooring, and simple baseboard and casings add historical character.

**LEFT:** IN SEARCH OF THE VIEW. The entries, stair, mudroom, and sitting room are located on the north side of the house (see the floor plan on the facing page) to buffer the living spaces from the road. The kitchen, dining, and living area runs along the south side of the house, and the sitting porch faces east across the valley. All of these spaces have views that span from the adjacent field to distant mountains.

Through Efficiency Vermont, we found Build Equinox, the company that developed the CERV—Conditioning Energy Recovery Ventilator. This refinement of the ERV provides fresh air from outside, circulates air within the house to maintain even temperature and humidity levels, monitors indoor air for key pollutants, and even has a small heater to temper the incoming fresh air.

## ENERGY TO SPARE

Although Karl Johnston had not yet built a net-zero-energy home, his reputation as a careful and thoughtful builder led us to choose him for this project. The owners also engaged Brent Mellen of Building Energy, a local insulation and energy-efficiency consulting company.

Achieving the air-barrier continuity over the transitions in materials and construction types was one of our significant challenges, and Brent was a big help in identifying practical strategies. For example, the underslab vapor barrier was lapped onto and taped to the foundation wall. Then at the top of the wall, a piece of poly sheeting was taped to the inside of the foundation, lapped over the top of the foundation, and taped to the plywood sheathing after the walls had been built.

**SECOND FLOOR**

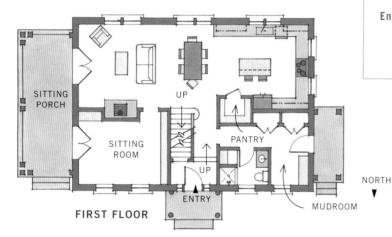

**FIRST FLOOR**

NORTH
▼

0    4    8         16 FT.

SPECS
**Bedrooms:** 3
**Bathrooms:** 3
**Size:** 2,240 sq. ft.
**Location:** Connecticut River Valley of Vermont
**Builder:** K.D. Johnston, Inc.
**Architect:** R. Andrew Garthwaite, AIA, hgarchitects.com
**Energy consultant:** Brent Mellen, Building Energy, buildingenergyvt.com

Thus, complete air-barrier continuity was achieved from below the slab to the top of the wall, with the second-floor ceiling providing the final link.

The weakest part of our air-sealing system is the woodstove. The owners loved the woodstove at their previous house, and it was important to them to include one. We were able to provide sealed combustion air to the firebox and decent air-sealing of the flue. In the end, the new house is so comfortable even in the depths of winter that Doug and Joan use the woodstove infrequently.

There were three blower-door tests. The first—a preinsulation test—was the most critical. We met our goal of less than 1 ACH50 at this early stage, and the two subsequent tests confirmed that we maintained our target as construction progressed.

In many ways, this house has functioned better than we all expected. It is warm, quiet, comfortable, and easy to operate. When the 9kw solar array was installed on the south-facing roof, the elec-

tric production resulted in an annual net surplus. Doug and Joan have been able to assign the excess power to family members living nearby. One lesson we learned is that during our cold winter's climate, it is best to turn the heat-pump water heater to standard electric-resistance heating; otherwise, it cools the basement.

Doug and Joan moved into the house in mid-November, just in time for a harsh New England winter. Shortly after they moved in, a severe overnight windstorm swept through the valley. Winds in excess of 60 mph blew shingles off the garage roof, but the house was so quiet that Doug and Joan didn't even realize that there had been a storm until the next morning. Every time the temperature hit a new low, I would email them to see how the house was doing. Every time, they replied that the house was warm and working as they had hoped. And with all the south-facing windows, sunny days are particularly pleasant, they said.

# RURAL LANDSCAPE, MODERN SENSIBILITY

A first-time home designer nails it with an updated farmhouse that includes double-duty spaces, a serious mudroom, and a five-star energy rating

BY DIANE KOLAK

FROM AN EARLY AGE, I DREAMED OF DESIGNING, my own home. My early creations, drawn on coated paper from the mill where my father worked, were sprawling, exotic, and modern. Walls of glass met at impractical angles, and there were many, many bathrooms. In every way, these imagined houses were different from the home of my youth in Michigan's rural Upper Peninsula, a simple farmhouse built by a Swedish immigrant in 1913.

Decades later, on a couple of wooded acres near Traverse City, Mich., I found myself imagining a home once again. My husband, Paul, and I had lived in a tiny apartment, then in our first home on a busy street in the city, and eventually in a nondescript trilevel in a rural neighborhood. These varied expressions of shelter helped us to develop a distinct idea of what we wanted—and didn't want—in a home of our own design.

I started reading books, sketching, and listing requirements: a flowing layout with long views through adjacent spaces, a first-rate mudroom, a window-filled kitchen, porches, a detached garage, thoughtful window placement, and a real connection to the outdoors. I wondered how my modern aesthetics could be reconciled with a house that fit our rural lot. Then I realized my Scandinavian ancestors had been doing that for a long time. Practical, efficient, and connected to nature, Scandinavian houses have an effortlessly modern elegance.

From that point, my sketches became more focused on a familiar, spare farmhouse structure, but with a streamlined edge. Paul and I visited the site on weekends to determine where best to place the house, roping off rooms and evaluating views, and figuring out the best way to route the driveway. We decided to set the house in the least picturesque area of the lot, a spot filled with weak second-growth poplars. I stood and imagined; I sketched and resketched.

With the site determined, I could begin to refine the shape and plan of the house. Nothing seemed just right. Then one night, while sketching on a coaster at a local brewpub, I hit upon a design that fused a two-story structure with a one-and-a-half-story structure roughly divided in half by a center stair (see the floor plan on p. 53). This became the key to situating all the rooms exactly where we wanted them in relation to the site and to each other.

A CONTEMPORARY FARMHOUSE. Fiber-cement siding painted with complementary colors and a roof composed of contrasting materials energize this classic image of home. The garage is a separate building, adding to the farm-compound look. Once her design came together on paper, the author built this foam-core model (left) to evaluate the composition.

## WHAT MAKES IT GREEN?

### STRUCTURE
- Icynene foam insulation creates an extremely tight structure, minimizing heat loss in winter and heat gain in summer.
- An insulated foundation and basement floor prevent significant heat loss.
- A whole-house electrostatic air-filtration and air-exchange system ensures fresh air and prevents moisture problems associated with a tightly insulated house.
- Low-e windows minimize heat transfer.
- Asphalt and metal roofing with a lifetime warranty are durable, keeping waste out of landfills.
- A detached garage keeps exhaust fumes out of the house.

### ELECTRICITY
- Energy Star appliances, CFL bulbs, and fluorescent cove lighting in the living and dining rooms lower energy consumption.

### WATER HEATING
- A tankless water heater saves energy by heating water on demand instead of maintaining a large tank of hot water.

### HEATING AND COOLING
- A geothermal heating and cooling system efficiently maintains physical and economic comfort.

### SUSTAINABLE FEATURES
- Low-VOC paints contribute to better air quality.
- Bamboo and cork flooring are made from rapidly renewable materials. There is no carpeting to trap allergens.
- MDF trim and interior doors save trees.
- Using recycled components, such as an antique pedestal sink, a screen door, and antique leaded-glass windows, extends their useful life and keeps them out of landfills.

- Bins for easy sorting of recyclables are built into the kitchen (photo above) and the mudroom. The homeowners recycle more than they throw away.
- Landscaping consists of ground cover, flowers, shrubs, and trees native to Michigan. The site has no turf; therefore, the homeowners use no fertilizers, no pesticides, and no lawn mower. In the fall, leaves are allowed to decay in place, mulching the plantings.

**FIRST FLOOR**

KITCHEN

DINING AREA

SCREENED PORCH

PASS-THROUGH

PANTRY

LIVING

UP

MUDROOM

GUEST ROOM

LAUNDRY CHUTE IN CEILING

NORTH

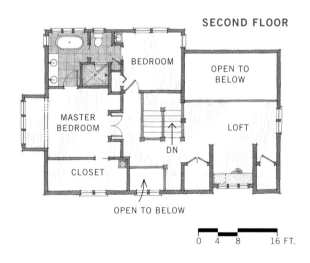

**SECOND FLOOR**

BEDROOM

OPEN TO BELOW

MASTER BEDROOM

LOFT

DN

CLOSET

OPEN TO BELOW

0  4  8  16 FT.

## OFFSET RECTANGLES ADD A DYNAMIC ELEMENT

At the entry, a 4-ft. jog in the floor plan makes room for a deep, welcoming front porch. In the foyer, the vestibule that leads to the powder room is sized to accommodate a future elevator. The side entrance leads to a multipurpose mudroom that includes the laundry and an elevated shower stall for parking muddy boots or washing the dog.

**SPECS**
**Bedrooms:** 3
**Bathrooms:** 2
**Size:** 2,350 sq. ft.
**HERS rating:** 53
**Location:** Lake Ann, Mich.
**Designer:** Diane Kolak
**Builder:** Steinorth Fine Homes,
steinorthfinehomes.com

## A 3-D MODEL TAKES ON A LEADING ROLE

I spent the following winter cutting and gluing foam-core walls and roofs to make a three-dimensional model of the house. It helped us solve some ceiling-height problems, and also allowed us to use a flashlight to mimic the path of the sun so that we could evaluate roof overhangs for summer shading and window placement for winter solar gain. Equally important, the model helped us to communicate our ideas to potential builders.

After talking with several, we met builders Mark and Jennifer Steinorth at their green model home in Traverse City. Immediately, we knew that we shared similar philosophies of design and craftsmanship, and we knew they understood our goals for the project. We turned our model and plans over to the Steinorths, who refined them and made suggestions to improve efficiency, structure, and budget use. They educated us and helped us to make as many green choices as our budget allowed (see the sidebar on the facing page). The completed house eventually earned a five-star Energy Star rating and green certification from the Home Builders Association of the Grand Traverse Area.

SCREENED-PORCH SLIDERS. Big glass doors between the porch and the living room allow the spaces to mingle when the weather is pleasant. Roof overhangs and deciduous trees shade the porch in summer. In winter, low-angled sunlight streams into the living room through the porch.

MULTIPURPOSE ROOM. Long diagonal views through the doors to the screened porch extend living-room sightlines. Slide open the barn door on the north wall, and the formal living room turns into a TV/family room.

## MULTIPURPOSE ROOMS ENRICH THE FLOOR PLAN

At 2,350 sq. ft., the house is smaller than average for our region, but I think it lives larger because many of the spaces do double duty. For example, we combined the more formal function of a living room with the informality of a family room by putting the TV in a closetlike recess covered with a barn-style door (see the photos above).

The guest room on the main floor is typically used as a library/game room. When guests arrive, we close off the foyer entrance to the three-quarter bath and allow them exclusive use of the bathroom.

Upstairs, the second bedroom is outfitted with an armoire that contains all my sewing gear and serves as a worksurface when opened up. For extra guests, we close the armoire and pump up an air bed. We installed a 1930s pedestal sink in the bed-

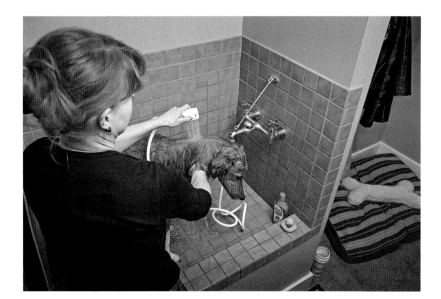

MUDROOM SHOWER. Next to the laundry, an elevated mini-shower stall makes a handy place to hang wet clothes, hose off muddy boots, or wash the dog.

room and provided access to the shower and toilet of the master bath via a pocket door, eliminating the need for a third bathroom in the house.

The loft space upstairs is very flexible. We decided that a built-in nook was adequate for our home office, rather than the extra room most house plans seem to include these days. The open space is great for exercising as well as for practicing our musical instruments. The vaulted ceilings have excellent acoustics.

The mudroom is a functional bonanza. In about 170 sq. ft., we have two closets; a dog shower/dirty-shoe washer/drip-dryer/plant-waterer; a washer/dryer and a folding counter; a hamper under the laundry chute from the master closet; space for the dog's bed and bowls, and a door to the outdoor kennel; built-in shelves for recycling and outdoor accessories; and a small counter space for sorting mail and all the other stuff that makes its way into the house. This room catches all the dirt and clutter, which makes it a lot easier to keep the rest of the house clean. Also, a nearby pantry takes pressure off storage space in the kitchen, freeing up wall space for windows.

We have lived in the house for a while now, and there are few things we would change. The electrical walk-through happened on a subzero day in March, resulting in some rushed decisions about switches and outlets that should have been better analyzed. And the landscaping is still a work in progress. We were shortsighted not to install geothermal heat from the start and have since converted to it (see the sidebar at right).

Considering the complexity of building a house, we're quite happy with the result. The key was allowing a lot of time for the design to evolve naturally, hiring a builder who understood us and our goals—and never losing sight of the home I pictured in my head.

## ENERGY-SMART SAVINGS WITH GEOTHERMAL HEAT

Because it cost more, we initially decided to forgo a geothermal heat-pump system in favor of a 95%-efficient propane furnace. Then fuel prices rose, and we realized our mistake. When calculations revealed that we could pay off a loan in four years based on the difference in operating costs for geothermal versus propane, we changed systems. As an added bonus, the geothermal system also keeps our house cool in summer.

In fact, our geothermal system saves money in several ways. The local utility company, Cherryland Electric Cooperative, encourages the use of geothermal as a smart energy alternative by discounting electric rates. They wire the geothermal heat pump to a separate meter and sell us that electricity at half price. In exchange, they have the option to shut down power to that meter should the system become overloaded. Since the utility began offering the program, they have never had to shut it down. But if it happens, our furnace still functions on propane as a backup. That is one advantage of having installed a conventional furnace, which we now use chiefly as an air handler.

During the first winter, we saved 70% on heating costs compared with the previous two winters. We went from an average of $90 a week for propane to $70 a month for electricity. Our house is also more comfortable because the system operates most efficiently by maintaining a constant temperature. There is no need to turn down the thermostat, so indoor air and surfaces maintain a comfortable temperature all the time.

# RESURRECTING A GREEK REVIVAL

After a dev-
astating fire
destroyed this
mid-1800s
home, the
owners and
architect
teamed up
to rebuild
a classic

BY PAUL HAGMAN

YEARS OF EXTENSIVE RESTORATION PERFORMED
by the owners of a mid-1800s Greek Revival house in the historic Village of
Poland, Ohio, came to a tragic end when a devastating fire broke out one
afternoon. While the fire destroyed the house beyond repair, it also ignited
a resilience within the owners to rebuild their home with the same degree
of care and craftsmanship they had put into restoring the original house.

The village of Poland is a study in traditional architecture, with
well-maintained examples of almost every house style of the 19th and
20th centuries. This house is situated near the former childhood home of
President William McKinley, and is surrounded by a variety of Italianate,
Second Empire, and colonial houses. One of the homeowners helped write
the village's historic preservation guidelines, so the couple understood
well the importance of preserving the character of the historic district.

After the owners decided to rebuild, a mutual friend put us in contact.
Although they had worked with other architects over the years during
renovations, this undertaking was of a different scale entirely. The homeowners wanted to remain faithful to the original home's style, proportions,
and siting, which took advantage of the gently rising lot and offered views
of nearby Yellow Creek. In one of our meetings, the owners shared with
me, "This community was so supportive during the renovation, and during
the loss, and that motivated us to build a home that honored the spirit and
character of our town."

## PLANNING MAKES PERFECT

Although rebuilding was unanticipated, the structural damage caused by
the fire left no other option. While the choice to design the new house
in a Greek Revival style seems an obvious one, the new house would not
just be a replica of the old. When the owners first approached me to help
with the project, it was unclear whether the interior layout should imitate
the layout of the former home or if a new approach should be taken to
suit modern living. The new build offered a unique opportunity to carefully reconsider the floor plan and to introduce modern conveniences and
building systems into a traditional-style home.

KEEPING IT CLASSIC. A respect for the historic charm of the neighborhood and the owners' original mid-1800s home inspired the owners and architect to rebuild in the classic Greek Revival style.

THE FRENCH-DOOR CONNECTION. The most-used spaces in the new house are the four-season room and the patio. These transitional spaces blend the interior and exterior and offer an ideal spot for year-round living. In the warm months, guests are able to take in views of the wooded rear lot and appreciate the fine landscaping from the patio, while the northeast Ohio winters are best appreciated from inside this cozy space.

After I analyzed the original home's floor plan, it became evident that the largest challenge in working with that plan was the centrally located staircase. This historic location of the stair, coupled with the modest size of the house, would have dictated the layout of all the other rooms and flexibility in the floor plan would have been severely limited. The solution to this problem was to move the staircase along the length of the house. The remaining space then became available for more creative planning to incorporate view corridors, a gallery wall, and unobstructed views across the creek to the park and historic village hall.

To add to the challenge, the previous home had received multiple renovations, additions, and reconfigurations over the years. The progressive changes were a part of its history and told a story about the people who lived there. Each alteration added a layer of interest that the owners appreciated and weren't eager to erase. Together we decided that a successful approach to the new home would include the appearance of having received additions over time, giving the home a more comfortable, broken-in presence in keeping with its village context.

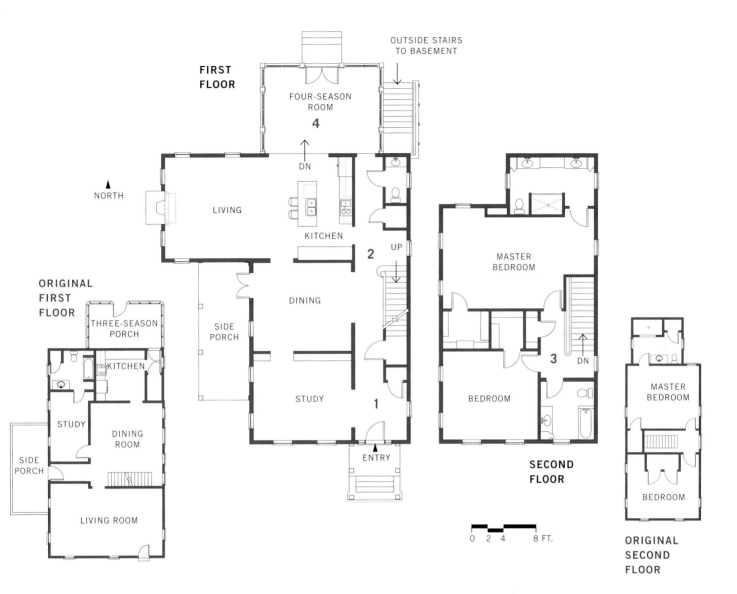

**FIRST FLOOR**

OUTSIDE STAIRS TO BASEMENT

FOUR-SEASON ROOM **4**

NORTH

DN

LIVING

KITCHEN

**2**

UP

DINING

**ORIGINAL FIRST FLOOR**

THREE-SEASON PORCH

KITCHEN

STUDY

DINING ROOM

SIDE PORCH

SIDE PORCH

LIVING ROOM

STUDY

**1**

ENTRY

MASTER BEDROOM

BEDROOM

**3**

DN

**SECOND FLOOR**

0  2  4      8 FT.

MASTER BEDROOM

BEDROOM

**ORIGINAL SECOND FLOOR**

**1** Guests coming in the house through the main entry now step into a formal entry foyer rather than directly into the living room.

**2** Locating the staircase along the length of the house instead of in the center allows rooms on the first floor to function better for today's more casual entertaining.

**3** Moving the staircase also improves the layout of the second floor. The L-shaped hallway leading to the guest and master bedrooms gives each more privacy. Each bedroom now has its own bath and walk-in closet.

**4** Updating the three-season porch to a four-season room and opening it up to the kitchen and living room creates an inviting space for entertaining.

**SPECS**
**Bedrooms:** 2
**Bathrooms:** 2½
**Size:** 2,495 sq. ft.
**Location:** Poland Village, Ohio
**Architect:** Paul Hagman, AIA, rbfcolab.com
**Builder:** Owner-built

FROM LITTLE BOX TO GREAT ROOM. No longer isolated from the rest of the house, the new kitchen space allows the homeowners to prepare meals and still enjoy interacting with guests.

## ATTENTION TO DETAIL

The process of creating the plans took several iterations, as spaces were arranged and rearranged on paper. A fully updated floor plan might better accommodate modern living but risked feeling too sterile, uninterrupted, or inauthentic. We experimented with the appropriate blend of individual rooms and open sightlines, always keeping the former home in mind. The fireplace was relocated several times to maintain views to the outdoors. The floor plan that finally emerged has a less formal arrangement of rooms. It places the focus on the kitchen, living room, and four-season room but still retains a formal dining room, study, and shotgun entry hall.

Because the owners wanted to maintain a historic feel, not only did we thicken the exterior wall for improved insulation, but we also gave visual heft to many interior walls by using 2x8 construction, offering a truer representation of common mid-1800s building practices. This also provided an opportunity for additional detail to wrap around the cased openings. In order to achieve accurate and pleasing proportions of the Greek Revival style, we carefully proportioned and dimensioned friezes and eave returns. The result is a warm home that

COZY LIVING YEAR-ROUND. Warmth is brought into the home through the rubble-stone-and-brick fireplace and carried throughout on the honey-colored, quartersawn white-oak flooring. The large cottage-sash windows allow in ample natural light, highlighting the hardwood floors.

acknowledges its traditional context, accommodates today's modern needs, and engages guests with delightful details.

Attention to construction methods and their impact on the environment were important from the outset. In addition to the 2x6 exterior-wall construction, the house was also wrapped in 2 in. of rigid insulation and taped before being clad. Raised-heel trusses were used throughout in order to achieve higher attic R-values, especially at the eaves where R-values often get reduced, causing ice dams in our region. We used low-e windows throughout the house, paid attention to careful sealing for air infiltration, and gave a lot of thought to natural lighting. We also installed a two-stage high-efficiency furnace and instant hot water heater to help even out the gas usage when demand isn't as great.

## CHARACTERISTICS OF GREEK REVIVAL HOMES

In wide use from the 1830s through the 1850s thanks to popular carpenters' pattern books, the Greek Revival style is a common sight through much of the eastern and midwestern regions where rapid settlement was occurring at that time.

The style is characterized by a low-pitched gable or hip roof and a strong frieze board, often with a high degree of symmetry along the primary facade.

Other details may include varying degrees of front-porch construction, from full-facade porches to the smaller entry porch shown on this home. The

porch is typically supported by columns or pilasters of a simple order.

Elaborate entry-door configurations and surrounds are a hallmark of the Greek Revival style. The exact execution of these details can vary regionally and from builder to builder, but narrow sidelights and transoms are typical of the door composition. Contrasting with the decorative entry are relatively simple window surrounds, which frame the 6-over-6 sashes common to the style.

## PATH TO SUCCESS

One should expect the planning and execution of a home as well crafted as this to take a bit longer than most homes. My experience shows that the best results come from a detailed set of plans and clear expectations developed in collaboration with the owners. This means taking the time to fully develop ideas and assess their suitability.

This project also benefited from the owners' hands-on approach to construction. Supervision of the construction process was undertaken by one of the homeowners, who, having grown up in a construction family, was able to make decisions and refinements along the way. When unforeseen circumstances arose that required changes, he was prepared.

Engaging with true craftsmen throughout the process yielded some exquisite details. Performance Homeworks meticulously executed the finish carpentry, from the three-piece stacked moldings to the authentic two-piece window casings manufactured by Baird Brothers Fine Hardwoods. Unique marble and subway-tile combinations in the master and guest baths were designed by the homeowners and installed by Aayers Flooring, which complement the custom bath and kitchen cabinetry by Pine Hollow Woodcraft. The exterior hemlock clapboard siding from Granville Manufacturing Company of Granville, Vt., frieze boards, and cornice work were expertly installed by CDT Construction Inc.

## THE STORY CONTINUES

The loss of the historic home was a tragedy, but elements of it persist. The original home's finely detailed portico and columns were salvaged to create a formal entryway for strangers and unexpected guests. The weighty front door was handcrafted by one of the owners using lumber salvaged from the original house. Horse-hitching stones and foundation stones salvaged from the fire were used as handsome accents on the patio. Although the historic home is no longer standing, with great dedication and skilled craftsmanship of their own, the owners honored each of the craftsmen who had a hand in shaping the former home while adding their own chapter to the story of the homestead.

# A NET-POSITIVE NEW ENGLAND FARMHOUSE

This new home blends the nostalgia of a traditional Massachusetts farmhouse with the needs of a 21st-century family

BY ROB WOTZAK

WHEN THEIR FAMILY OUTGREW THE COZY 1850s home they had meticulously renovated, Mark and Pilar Doughty were faced with the choice of buying and renovating a roomier historic house or building a new home. They felt that energy efficiency, comfort, and environmental responsibility were essential requirements, and after a few years of house hunting and number crunching it became clear that building a new custom home would be the smartest way to get everything their family needed and wanted.

Renovating and living in an old New England farmhouse prepared the Doughtys for planning their ideal home, but it was still a daunting task. Fortunately, as president of Thoughtforms, a cutting-edge custom home builder in the Boston area, Mark had experience managing the construction of many energy-efficient homes—but he had never been involved with a build this modest, nor one this personal. To make their dream home a reality, the Doughtys enlisted the help of like-minded architecture firm ZeroEnergy Design (ZED). Mark had met the design team at ZED years ago, but hadn't found an opportunity to work with them until now. "We were impressed with their passion, their integrated architecture and engineering, and their commitment to sustainable design," Mark remembers. ZED managing director Stephanie Horowitz felt that Mark and Pilar were ideal clients because they brought with them an extensive knowledge of houses but were honest about the limits of their own expertise.

The design team used an iterative approach to create a plan that matched the way the Doughtys wanted to live in their home. Stephanie noted that it's common for ZED to alternate between trying to tease out what a client is looking for and offering concepts they've had success with in past projects. Everyone spent a great deal of time discussing details such as how the family expected to move through the house and how they and their guests would interact within the various spaces. The resulting plan is a hybrid, reminiscent of the antique homes Mark and Pilar are so fond of, but with features added or omitted to better match their contemporary way of life.

## AN INFORMAL ENTRY

The Doughtys opted to make the mudroom their main entry, forgoing the formal front door common to nearly every old New England home. Without the expense of the additional porch and door, Mark and Pilar felt comfortable splurging for a Belgian bluestone mudroom floor, which appealed to them for its durability, its rugged good looks, and its ability to

OUTDOOR CONNECTION. The detached garage encourages the homeowners to spend more time appreciating their natural surroundings. The breezeway serves multiple purposes: protecting the entrance from the elements, easing passage between the front yard and backyard, and providing a cozy spot for a porch swing. There is no front door; instead, the homeowners opted to have all exterior doors lead to their private outdoor spaces.

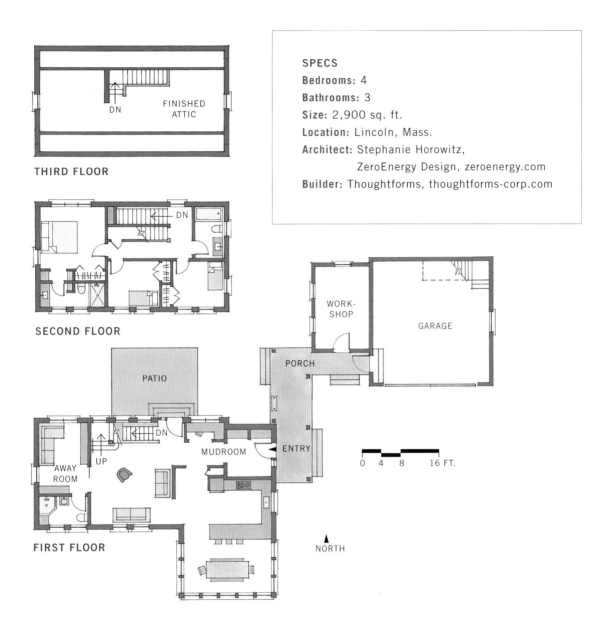

THIRD FLOOR

SECOND FLOOR

FIRST FLOOR

FINISHED ATTIC

DN

SPECS
Bedrooms: 4
Bathrooms: 3
Size: 2,900 sq. ft.
Location: Lincoln, Mass.
Architect: Stephanie Horowitz,
ZeroEnergy Design, zeroenergy.com
Builder: Thoughtforms, thoughtforms-corp.com

WORK-SHOP
GARAGE
PORCH
PATIO
DN
UP
MUDROOM
ENTRY
AWAY ROOM

0  4  8        16 FT.

NORTH

hide dirt tracked in on the kids' sneakers. The rest of the main floors are rustic white oak, complete with knots and country charm.

The mudroom opens into the bright main floor, leading to a compact office alcove on the right, the kitchen and dining area on the left, and straight into the living room through the center of the house. Activities in the living room can overflow into a multipurpose away room on the far side of the house—but slide a pair of pocket doors closed and the away room, along with its adjacent full bathroom, becomes a private guest suite.

Even though it's nestled into one corner of the first floor, the kitchen and its accompanying dining area is the heart of the home. It's also one of the brightest and cheeriest rooms, with a row of extra-large corner windows making it feel almost as though you're sitting outside. Shaker-style cherry cabinets add warmth to the room and are a nod to the nearly identical cabinets the Doughtys loved in their previous home.

The compact, interconnected first-floor plan allows the Doughtys and their children to be together and interact even when engaging in differ-

THREE FLOORS, USED WELL. One of the homeowners' favorite features is the natural light that fills the entire house. The brightly lit kitchen is more than just the heart of the home—it's large triple-pane windows soak up heat on sunny winter days and let cool breezes blow through in warmer months. There is a small space between the stair and the wall to allow light to fill the first floor (photo at left).

ent activities. "The design has fully supported our daily routines and the values that we have around family, togetherness, and space," Pilar asserts. The second-floor plan is much more traditional. The two kids' rooms share a bathroom and all of the rooms—including the master suite—are modest in size by today's standards.

Head up one more flight of stairs and you'll find one of the family's favorite living spaces. Because of its openness and simplicity, the Doughtys find that they use the finished attic for any number of activities that don't have dedicated places elsewhere in the house. Pilar acknowledges the obvious use of the attic as a playroom, as a craft room, and as an extra sleeping space for guests, but she also says the attic hosts uncommon activities such as breakdancing and practicing Reiki.

## OUTSIDE, A MIX OF TRADITIONAL AND UNCOMMON IDEAS

The house and garage are both simple two-story structures with steep gable roofs and unfinished wood siding—details that are common to the New England vernacular. The barnlike detached garage, with its open breezeway leading to the house, evokes regional country homes from a time before automobiles and heated garages. But the Doughtys' primary reason for keeping the garage separate from the house is to encourage themselves to appreciate their natural surroundings every day.

There are two prominent exterior features that clearly diverge from the traditional aesthetic so prevalent throughout the house. The most apparent is the tidy array of solar panels that almost completely covers the front half of the roof. The second unusual feature is the bump-out, which flanks the right corner of the house. Though it does look similar to an enclosed porch, its large windows, its front-and-center location, and the bold asymmetry it adds to the façade are distinctly modern elements that ZED introduced to bring the entrance down in scale and to allow for more generous windows in the dining area.

## GETTING TO NET-POSITIVE

Because of ZED's commitment to energy efficiency, their team always comes to the table with a list of performance specifications as non-negotiable items. Details like size, layout, and finish materials can be adjusted, but not envelope details or HVAC systems.

Jordan Goldman, ZED engineering principal, pointed out that Thoughtforms typically builds much larger homes, so Mark and Pilar had purchasing connections not usually available for such a modest project. This, paired with ZED's capabilities for cost analysis and performance modeling, led to impressive energy efficiency.

ZED penned a time-tested building envelope that Jordan is comfortable calling a ZED standard assembly. It starts with conventional 2x6 framing. Dense-pack cellulose on the inside and two layers of 2-in. rigid foam on the outside make it super-insulated. The roof is similarly insulated, but with three layers of 2-in. foam and enough cellulose to fill the rafter bays. A meticulously sealed weather barrier helped the house become among the most airtight in the country, with a final air-leakage level of 0.27 ACH50.

Overall, the house performs better than anticipated, largely due to the Doughtys' conscientious efforts to conserve energy. The 13.8kw photovoltaic array produces 50% more power than the family currently uses, which will allow enough capacity to charge an electric car in the future. In the meantime, Mark and Pilar are happy to collect a check from their utility company for the surplus energy.

The benefits are equally about comfort. "In our old 1850s house," Pilar recalls, "we were constantly pulling shades up and down to regulate cooling in the summer and wearing knit caps in the winter to stay warm without breaking the bank." The new house is always the right temperature.

And Mark pointed out one more pleasant surprise that's made him proud: During a particularly severe New England blizzard a year after the house was built, there wasn't a single icicle hanging from the eaves.

## SPECS AT A GLANCE

### PERFORMANCE

ENERGY-USE INTENSITY: -6.3 kBtu per sq. ft. annually (net positive)

AIR LEAKAGE: 0.27 ACH50

### SYSTEMS

RENEWABLE ENERGY: 13.8kw solar electric system

AIR BARRIER UNDER SLAB: 10-mil poly

AIR BARRIER AT WALL AND ROOF SHEATHING: Solitex Mento 1000 membrane taped with Tescon Vana

WINDOWS: Makrowin MW88 wood triple-pane tilt-turn windows (U-0.15; SHGC 0.32)

HEATING AND COOLING: Mitsubishi MXZ-8B48NA air-source heat pump

VENTILATION: Zehnder ComfoAir 550 ERV

HOT WATER: Stiebel Eltron Accelera 300 heat-pump water heater

# A GO-TO ASSEMBLY

For the team at ZeroEnergy Designs, this building assembly is a proven performer.

### R-69 ROOF CONSTRUCTION

To achieve the high R-value of this roof, the assembly includes polyiso insulation above the roof deck and cellulose insulation in the rafter cavities. The metal standing-seam roofing is fastened to an additional 1/2-in. layer of plywood sheathing installed above the exterior rigid foam. Inside, the ceiling plasterboard is installed over 1x3 strapping and finished with no-VOC primer and paint.

### R-44 WALL CONSTRUCTION

This wall assembly has 4 in. of foil-faced poly-iso rigid insulation with staggered and taped seams outside. The exterior foam adds R-value and is used to minimize thermal bridging. The siding is fastened to 3/4-in. furring strips, creating a space for drainage and airflow. The interior walls are also finished with no-VOC primer and paint.

### R-36 FOUNDATION WALL CONSTRUCTION

To keep the basement dry, the concrete wall has liquid-applied waterproofing and a drainage mat. The basement is insulated inside with 4 in. of foil-faced polyiso rigid insulation sealed to concrete and unfaced batt insulation in the wall cavities. The 5/8-in. moisture-resistant plasterboard is finished with no-VOC primer and paint.

### R-26 SLAB CONSTRUCTION

Air movement and vapor are controlled under the slab with 10-mil poly that wraps up at the slab edge and is taped to the foundation wall. The slab is insulated with 6-in. EPS rigid insulation that wraps up the slab edge to break the thermal bridge.

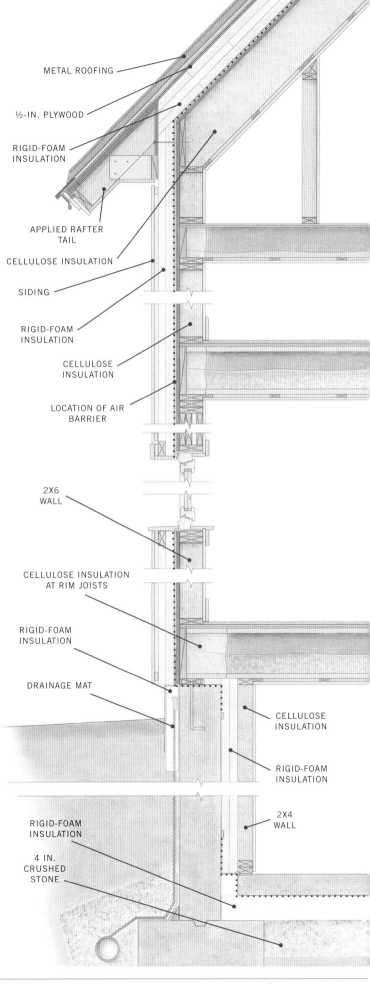

METAL ROOFING

1/2-IN. PLYWOOD

RIGID-FOAM INSULATION

APPLIED RAFTER TAIL

CELLULOSE INSULATION

SIDING

RIGID-FOAM INSULATION

CELLULOSE INSULATION

LOCATION OF AIR BARRIER

2X6 WALL

CELLULOSE INSULATION AT RIM JOISTS

RIGID-FOAM INSULATION

DRAINAGE MAT

RIGID-FOAM INSULATION

4 IN. CRUSHED STONE

CELLULOSE INSULATION

RIGID-FOAM INSULATION

2X4 WALL

# REINVENTING THE FARMHOUSE

An architect
uses the site
itself to guide
his take on
a traditional
style

BY ROB WHITTEN

RIMMED ON THE NORTH BY A MIXED FOREST, the wide grassy field fell gently to the south, toward the road we'd taken to where we now stood. As a home site, the field in front of us promised the best solar gain you could ask for in this part of Maine, along with ample drainage, protection from north winds, and stunning views. It was a site that couldn't miss—whether you were a 19th-century farmer or a 21st-century architect.

I happen to be the latter. But when I laid out my plans for the site to Steve and Deb—the potential clients whom I had met that day in the field—I spoke as if I were that farmer. My firm would design their house on the slope toward the north, not the center, of that beautiful meadow. The tall side would face south, and the driveway would snake off into the trees to the northeast, because no self-respecting farmer would cut a road through the middle of a good field.

In a more timeless sense, what I was saying was that you don't place your house on the best land—you place it adjacent to the best land, to establish a relationship with it. This application of centuries of local wisdom appealed to Steve and Deb, and our conversation that day was just the beginning of a dialogue about how best to incorporate that knowledge into the building of their comfortable, durable, and contemporary farmhouse.

## DOWNSIZING DONE RIGHT

When they first decided to downsize, Steve and Deb considered buying an old house. But then a piece of land they had admired for years came on the market. They started assembling a virtual catalog of what they liked and didn't like in a house, and they reached out to a few local design-build firms and a few architects, myself included.

In true Yankee tradition, Steve and Deb were looking for straightforward answers and good value in the design of their new home. The traditional approach I described that morning appealed to them, so with a clear understanding of their budget and their design goals, I got the job. As the design developed, I was joined by Whitten Architects team member Will Fellis, who comes from a long line of Maine builders and has both an innate and a trained understanding of local building traditions.

FACING THE SUN. The farmhouse faces south for maximum solar gain, with the porch overhangs affording cooling shade in summer. A wide farmer's porch is a traditional feature of a New England farmhouse, though the everyday entrance here is around the back.

## A FARMHOUSE EVOLVES

FROM THE RIGHT SITE . . .
It's typical today to plop a home directly in the center of a site, but a
more traditional—and wiser—approach is to consider solar orientation,
wind direction, drainage, and the desirability of preserving the best land
(for farming in the past, for the view in the present). Those factors led the
author to position this contemporary farmhouse in the far northeast corner
of the site, near the top of a rise. While the house faces south toward the
sun, the barnlike garage is angled to allow the driveway to curve off into
the trees at the edge of the site, preserving the meadow and the view.

## . . . TO THE ARRIVAL SEQUENCE

How one approaches the house—from the driveway, into the dooryard, and then inside—informs the organization of doors, service areas, and ultimately, the floor plan (shown on p. 80). A farmhouse is an informal country home; to enter and exit, everyone uses the back door and the mudroom entry. The front door is used to access the front porch and is placed in the ceremonial, front-and-center location.

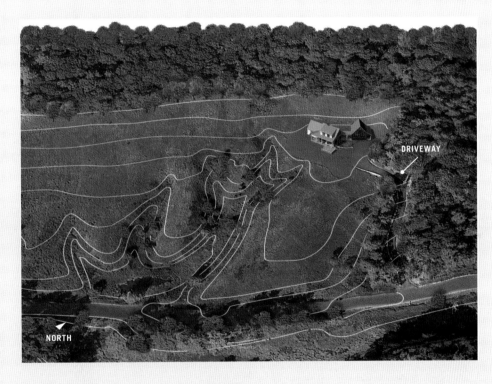

ON HIGHER GROUND. Positioning the house on an elevated corner of the property preserved the character of the large parcel of land and enhanced the owners' southern views over the undulating terrain.

The second step I always take before designing a new home is to visit the clients' current house. This accomplishes two things. First, it reveals why the first house doesn't work. Second, it enables me to design spaces that will accommodate the clients' furniture and lifestyle. My visit revealed why Steve and Deb had struggled with their last house.

Although 2,900 sq. ft., it was poorly organized, so much of the space was unused. Steve and Deb were clear that they wanted a house of no more than 2,500 sq. ft., with a first-floor master, a hardworking mudroom, and a home office that would be, in Sarah Susanka's language, an "away space." They wanted this to be their lifetime house.

## FROM SITE TO SPACES

When I design a house, I start with the site plan. I use that to develop the floor plan, which in turn shapes the house's overall form. In a sense, this follows the tradition of New England farmhouses, which are essentially simple, efficient boxes encasing a floor plan suited to their site. In choosing that site, 19th-century builders thought first about the sun, then about the wind, and then about proper drainage. Their time and effort were not put into making a palace, but a house that worked with the land.

In those days, building on a slope was favored because it meant less digging, which was done by hand. We took a similar approach, tucking the house into the land in a traditional manner. Building this way also allows runoff to drain away from the foundation—in this case, aided by a perimeter-drain system we installed uphill from the house.

Like those old farmers, our goal was a house of modest scale. The modern-day challenge, however, is that once you attach a garage, you end up with a huge appendage that represents almost a third of your footprint. The answer is to move the two apart. In Maine, a sheltered outdoor space between the house and garage or barn where you do your work is referred to as a dooryard. There is a tradition in Maine of dooryard visits, in which neighbors pull up to the house and roll down the window to chat with whoever is working there.

Following this arrival sequence—from the car, to the mudroom, to the service spaces, to living and dining areas, and finally, to more private spaces— enables the floor plan to evolve naturally. To make the most of 2,500 sq. ft., we turned to an open plan in which public spaces were shared. I always begin by laying out the first floor, which tells me where the stair wants to be, which in turn brings me to the second floor. I want the second-floor bedrooms to be facing the sun, so they fall into place next. I also like the bedrooms to have windows on two walls for ample light and cross ventilation.

FROM YARD TO DOOR. The so-called dooryard area that stretches from the front of the barn toward the house is the starting point for arrival and influences the position of the mudroom, the back entry, and the kitchen.

## DEVELOPING THE FLOOR PLAN

The arrival sequence continues inside the house, determining the layout of the first floor and then the second while also taking into account the house's orientation. Utility spaces are located on the darker north side, which is separated from the south-facing living and dining spaces (photos facing page) by the hall and the stairway. Although located on the main floor, the master bedroom is buffered from public spaces by the home office, the laundry room, and the walk-in closet.

0   4   8          16 FT.

DOORYARD

UP

LAUNDRY   MUDROOM

SITTING AREA

ENTRY

KITCHEN

UP

DN

MASTER
BEDROOM

BEDROOM   BEDROOM

LIVING      DINING

OFFICE

ENTRY

SCREENED PORCH

FARMER'S PORCH

**FIRST FLOOR**

**SECOND FLOOR**

SPECS
**Bedrooms:** 3
**Bathrooms:** 2½
**Size:** 2,500 sq. ft.
**Cost:** $275 per sq. ft.
**Completed:** 2013
**Location:** Freeport, Maine
**Architect:** Whitten Architects, Portland, Maine; whittenarchitects.com
**Builder:** Rousseau Builders, rousseaubuilders.com
**Interior designer:** Krista Stokes, kristastokes.com

**TOP:** ARRIVING AT HOME. The mudroom entrance, used by family and friends alike, leads into the kitchen, which is also positioned with a view toward the driveway.

**ABOVE:** TRADITIONAL TOUCH. In the living room, the modified Rumford fireplace is taller and more efficient than a typical fireplace. The built-in firewood box offers a historic reference to a traditional New England beehive oven, but with more functionality.

SMOOTH LANDING. At the top of the stairs, a small landing becomes a private space for guests, who also use the upstairs bedrooms.

## A FORM UNFOLDS

With the interior spaces in place, the form of the house begins to reveal itself. It is shaped by the rooms inside and by the character of the area. Steve and Deb's home site is located just outside the village of Freeport. The area is full of smaller-scale houses built from the 1780s to 1900, offering a traditional frame of reference.

Because this house was situated outside the village, I believed that a farmhouse form would be most appropriate. We were drawn to the Cape style, with a raised dormer facing the sun and an unbroken roof slanted against the north winds. To me, this represented a type of small and simple house with the economical patterns we wanted. I used pitches of 11-in-12 on the main roof and a gentler 5-in-12 on the roofs of the porch, the breezeway, and the dormer. The pitch of the master wing falls between them at 8-in-12 and is offset 2 ft. from the north wall of the house. It adds character and

scale, and it suggests that the master wing was a later addition by the "farmer."

Now it was time to think about windows. We confined our windows to four types, the most prominent being two-over-one double hungs and four-lite casements. Each of the upper lites matches the proportion of the window overall, creating a harmony to the way the pieces come together that's both spare and refined at the same time.

With windows and doors in place, we moved outside to add the transitional spaces—porches, patios, and shelters—that complete the connection between what's inside and what's outside. Those include a covered walkway to protect the route from the garage to the mudroom, and a 6-ft.-wide farmer's porch to shelter the front door and to provide protected, outdoor living space. Beyond the porch, we planned a fieldstone wall to enclose a stone terrace and fire pit.

THE FINAL FORM. Once the interior spaces are organized, transitional spaces linking them with the outdoors can be established. Those include a wide farmer's porch, a screened porch off the home office, a terrace and fire pit just off the farmer's porch, and a covered walkway connecting the house to the garage.

Steve and Deb already had stretched their budget, so we wanted to keep the exterior simple. Steve and Deb also valued low maintenance, so we invested in a standing-seam Galvalume roof, prefinished Maibec white-cedar shingles (installed over a drainage gap), and prefinished board-and-batten siding for the garage. Trim and corner details are thin and Shaker-like, which helped keep material costs in check.

## HIGH PERFORMANCE, THEN AND NOW

Built to relate to the land, sun, and climate, a traditional farmhouse was the high-performance, low-cost house of its day. We used those wonderful vernacular lessons because they work, but we also included some more recent technologies to boost this house's efficiency.

We used ZIP System sheathing over 2x6 walls insulated with 4 in. of closed-cell spray foam (R-30); rafter bays under the ZIP-sheathed roof are insulated to R-49 with 8 in. of closed-cell spray foam. (Closed-cell foam is derived from petrochemicals, but we decided that its ability to lower the home's energy demand balanced out the environmental penalty involved in its manufacture.)

The outside of the foundation and the underside of the basement slab are insulated with 2 in. of rigid foam (R-10). Our last blower-door test put airtightness at 0.36 ACH50, thanks to carefully detailed wall and roof assemblies, taped sheathing, spray foam, and a meticulous framing crew. Tight houses need a source of fresh air, so Steve chose a heat-recovery ventilation system that exhausts from the bathroom and kitchen area, with supplies to the first-floor bedroom and living spaces.

Harboring a Yankee bias against overdependence on someone else, Steve settled on a closed-loop geothermal heating system utilizing a Bosch two-stage ground-source heat pump and a desuperheater with electric backup for domestic hot water. We also built a chase through the house that will enable Steve and Deb to install photovoltaics on the master-suite roof when their budget allows.

As the house neared completion, we received emails and comments from neighbors and passersby telling us how much they loved the way it looked in the field. It was gratifying to know that we were being seen not only as good neighbors but as responsible stewards of a very special piece of land.

# FARMHOUSE, PASSIVE HOUSE

This compact farmhouse achieves home building's highest performance standard without a shred of aesthetic compromise

BY JUSTIN PAULY

AFTER BOTH GROWING UP IN CALIFORNIA, Mica and Laureen lived together in many other places throughout their busy careers. Their hearts have always been on the West Coast, though, and they longed to return one day. They eventually found a small piece of property in the coastal enclave of Carmel-by-the Sea on the Monterey Peninsula, and they hired me as architect and Rob Nicely of Carmel Building & Design as builder for a new house that would be their permanent home. The collaboration yielded a new type of house for this area, one that appropriately breaks free of the local vernacular while also meeting the country's most aggressive performance benchmarks.

This Passive House was a first for Rob, for me, and for the city of Carmel. Working on this project has confirmed for Rob and me the importance of sustainable, high-performance design and building. For the city and for those who now get to experience this home, I hope the house evokes a realization that design and performance can be held to the same very high standard and that beautiful, exceptionally low-energy homes are within our collective reach.

## A FEAR OF PASSIVE HOUSE

One of the initial challenges with our project was providing Mica and Laureen with the house that they wanted while also convincing Carmel's strict planning commission that the project would complement the existing city fabric. When we first sent the project to the commission, we were so excited about the idea of building Carmel's first Passive House that we included a Passive House brochure. Unfortunately, that decision had the opposite effect of what we hoped. Instead of getting people excited about our project, it scared them into thinking that we were going to build a box with a wall of south-facing glass and few other openings. While this design might be true of some Passive Houses, our plans called for a different home. Mica and Laureen wanted a contemporary farmhouse with a clean, crisp, and inviting exterior, and an interior with an open floor plan that would use a series of outdoor spaces to create a strong relationship with the small yet dramatic site. Fortunately, the commission was able to see that vision, and our plans were approved.

CENTER STAGE. With its dramatic vaulted ceiling and massive timbered fan trusses, the dining area occupies the middle of the house (photo left). A large bay window floods the space with light from the south, while French doors open the house to the red-woods and patio to the north (photo above).

FARMHOUSE LIVING. The living room sits beneath a whitewashed Douglas-fir ceiling and before whitewashed Douglas-fir plank walls and custom built-ins. Separated from the grand dining space by only a double-sided fireplace, the living room is very much connected to the hub of the house, while affording respite from the activity within it.

## WORKING AROUND THE REDWOODS

The lot is a 4,000-sq.-ft. flag-shaped parcel hemmed in on three sides by existing homes and on the fourth side by a cluster of massive redwood trees. These redwoods are the dominant feature on the property and became the inspiration for many of the house's design decisions.

The lot's physical and regulatory constraints led us to position most of the house at the rear of the property, with a small single-car garage placed at the street. The garage is linked to the house via a narrow, covered breezeway that steps down slightly to accommodate a subtle change in topography across the site. We placed a small courtyard directly behind the redwood trees and in front of

## EVOKING COMFORT IN AN OPEN PLAN

The floor plan has carefully designed spaces for gathering and retreat. The core of the plan is the vaulted dining room, which brings people together in the heart of the home. More intimate spaces branch off this central space and are enriched with elements that make them inviting and comfortable.

SPECS

**Bedrooms:** 2
**Bathrooms:** 2½
**Size:** 1,600 sq. ft.
**Location:** Carmel, Calif.
**Architect:** Justin Pauly, paulydesigns.com
**Builder:** Rob Nicely, carmelbuilding.com

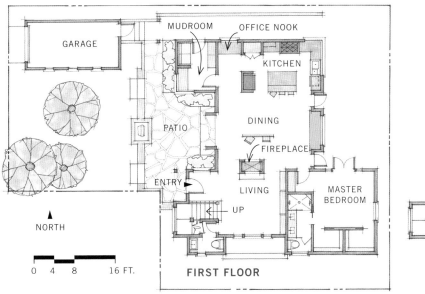

NORTH

0  4  8    16 FT.

FIRST FLOOR

SECOND FLOOR

the main living space, and a more private outdoor area directly to the south of the main living space at the rear of the property. The garage and breezeway give the property a "compound" feel, while the outdoor areas tie the interior spaces to the exterior site and help to give the compact house a needed sense of openness.

## OPEN SPACES AND INTIMATE PLACES

In addition to well-connected indoor and outdoor spaces, Mica and Laureen also requested a well-designed kitchen with a large open space nearby for entertaining and smaller, more intimate spaces for relaxing and reading. The compact kitchen and mudroom lie to the north of the dining room; to

the south are a small sitting room, a powder room, a master bedroom, and stairs to the second-floor suite. While the vaulted dining room, with large openings to the north and south, lends the house a sense of grandeur, all of the other rooms have a more intimate feel because of their smaller footprint and warm, natural finishes.

## A TWIST ON A TRADITIONAL STYLE

Many of the interior and exterior spaces include traditional elements rendered in more modern detail. Inside, a palette of exposed whitewashed rough-sawn Douglas-fir framing, integral colored plaster, and floorboards made of reclaimed barn wood adds to the warmth of the spaces. Board-

and-batten detailing on the upper portion of the fireplace and a large sliding barn door in the upstairs bedroom continue to reinforce the farmhouse aesthetic.

We covered the exterior in white board-and-batten siding that sits atop a continuous water table, with lap siding below to offer a sense of grounding to the home's base. We chose standing-seam zinc-coated metal for the roof, with clear cedar trim for the fascia and underside of the eaves. This boxed-in eave detail gives the whole lid the clean feel of a separate element that has been dropped neatly onto the home below. Additionally, the large cedar sliding barn doors and the exaggerated scale of the foursquare window at the stairwell on the north elevation are prominent elements that push the house's style toward the contemporary.

## SLASHING ENERGY USE

The Passive House approach to building hinges on minimizing the amount of energy consumed in a home by providing extremely high levels of insulation and minimizing air leakage. Unlike other rating systems and certification programs, Passive House

HALF-BATH. With a Duravit sink atop a custom walnut stand set under a Troy pendant, even the bright, airy half-bath off the living room reinforces elegant farmhouse simplicity.

GUEST SUITE. In the small bedroom, a sliding barn door with an operable window helps to define the home's farmhouse style and creates privacy at the top of the stairs.

tends to focus wholly on energy consumption, which has long been a concern for Rob and me.

Several design strategies helped the house to achieve its performance goals. The compact footprint is a key attribute of a super-low-energy building. Furthermore, we maximized the amount of solar gain in the main living areas of the house through generous amounts of southern glazing. Passive Houses tend to minimize the amount of glazing on their north sides, which typically bleed energy without providing any positive solar gain. In the case of this house, however, eliminating windows and doors on the north side would have changed the entire look and feel of the home.

Fortunately, we were able to compensate for the large glazed openings to the north by using more insulation in the walls and roof. A combination of advanced-framing techniques and what we

consider a "dual-skinned" construction approach to the roof and walls gave us a well-insulated envelope and enabled us to hit our blower-door targets. If the house performs as modeled, it will use approximately 15% to 20% of the energy consumed by a code-built house.

Our mechanical system is comprised of a Zehnder heat-recovery ventilator (HRV) that serves two purposes. First, it provides a continuous flow of fresh air into the house. Second, it uses warm indoor air to preheat fresh makeup air through a heat-exchange core to minimize overall heat losses. A hydronic coil added to the HRV serves as a backup heating element. With the obvious exception of certain duct runs, the entire mechanical system lives in a fairly conventional crawlspace under the house. This design detail meant that we had to forgo a concrete slab, which is often used in Passive

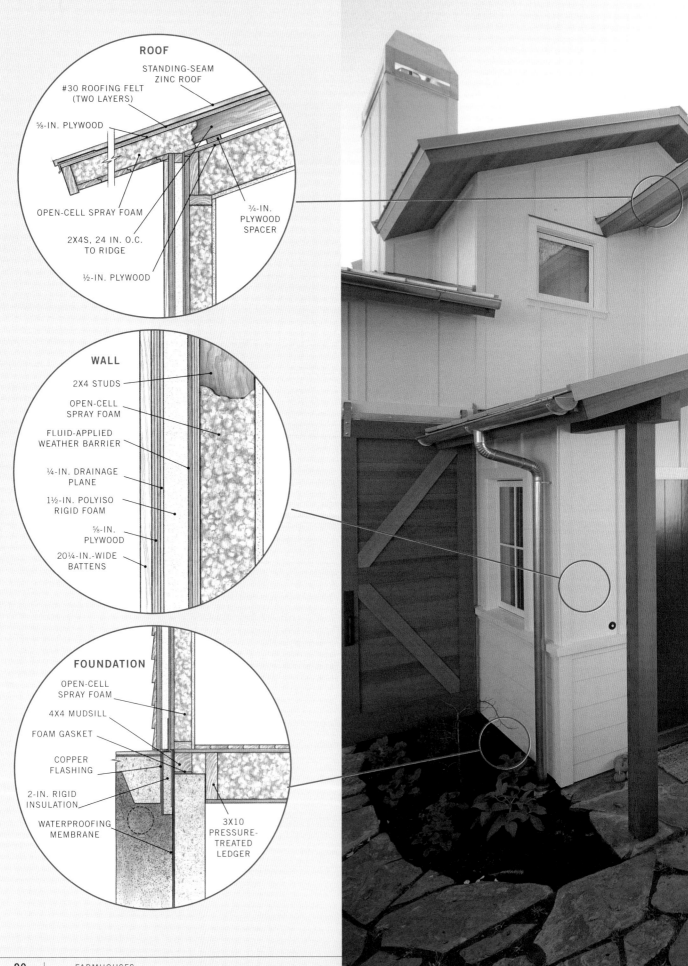

**ROOF**

STANDING-SEAM ZINC ROOF

#30 ROOFING FELT (TWO LAYERS)

⅝-IN. PLYWOOD

OPEN-CELL SPRAY FOAM

2X4S, 24 IN. O.C. TO RIDGE

½-IN. PLYWOOD

¾-IN. PLYWOOD SPACER

**WALL**

2X4 STUDS

OPEN-CELL SPRAY FOAM

FLUID-APPLIED WEATHER BARRIER

¼-IN. DRAINAGE PLANE

1½-IN. POLYISO RIGID FOAM

⅝-IN. PLYWOOD

20¼-IN.-WIDE BATTENS

**FOUNDATION**

OPEN-CELL SPRAY FOAM

4X4 MUDSILL

FOAM GASKET

COPPER FLASHING

2-IN. RIGID INSULATION

WATERPROOFING MEMBRANE

3X10 PRESSURE-TREATED LEDGER

## COMPONENTS FOR CONSERVATION

This home consumes as little energy as possible and holds onto that energy for as long as possible through a well-designed envelope. All of the major components have been detailed to ensure optimum performance, while being practical to build.

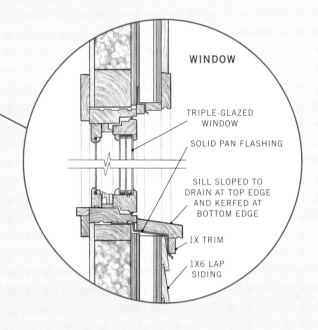

**WINDOW**

TRIPLE-GLAZED WINDOW

SOLID PAN FLASHING

SILL SLOPED TO DRAIN AT TOP EDGE AND KERFED AT BOTTOM EDGE

1X TRIM

1X6 LAP SIDING

Houses to store solar energy. As an alternative, we incorporated phase-change materials (PCMs) into the wall assemblies on the south side of the house to serve as a thermal heat sink. PCMs help to regulate indoor temperatures by absorbing excess heat during the day and slowly releasing the heat in the evenings, when the interior temperature dips below the 73°F set point. PCMs simply install as sheets behind the drywall of the interior walls.

Other than the use of PCMs, the construction of this house was intentionally straightforward. I hope that many of the design and construction techniques we used will become mainstream in the years ahead and that high-performance houses such as this will become synonymous with high-end construction.

# A BETTER, HEALTHY HOME

This practical and healthy home confronts the challenges of location, extreme weather, climate change, and the looming clean-water crisis

BY BRIAN PONTOLILO

ACCORDING TO NASA, THE DECADE FROM 2009 TO 2019 was the hottest decade ever recorded, and 2015 was the third hottest of those 10 years. But climate change is fickle, and during the winter of 2015, many in the northeastern United States were muttering the new cliché, "So much for global warming!" Instead of experiencing the warm winter much of the western United States was having, the northeastern states were bundling up against the polar vortex, the extremely cold pocket of air that typically hovers above the Arctic but occasionally reaches deeper into North America.

That winter, Margate, N.J., had its third-coldest February since 1895. Frigid temperatures caused Kirsten and Joe Levin's heat pump to fail. "I don't remember how long it was before we realized the heat wasn't working," says Kirsten, "but it took a while." Once they figured out that the temperature in their new house had dropped a few degrees, Kirsten plugged in a pair of small electric space heaters that she had used to help heat the uninsulated cottage that formerly occupied the property. "We were fine," she says. "It's amazing how well the new house holds heat."

It's said that a certified Passive House can be heated with a couple of hair dryers, but Kirsten and Joe's home is not a Passive House. It is certified by the New Jersey Climate Choice Home program, which means that it meets New Jersey Energy Star requirements. But for the team at ZeroEnergy Design (ZED) responsible for designing it, such certifications are a means to financial incentives—namely, rebates—not a goal in and of themselves or necessarily a performance standard.

Architect Stephanie Horowitz, engineer Jordan Goldman, and business-development director Adam Prince started ZED with a simple commitment: to design houses and other buildings that use 50% less energy than those built to code. Yet Kirsten and Joe's home has much more to offer than a tight, well-insulated envelope: It fits well into its eclectic neighborhood, it is sited to maximize opportunities for light and outdoor space, it conserves water, it is designed and built to stand up to coastal storms and flooding, it has finish materials and mechanical systems that support its owners' physical health, and it has a floor plan that supports the family's lifestyle.

With four bedrooms and three baths in 2,600 sq. ft., this home is similar to the average new American home described by the U.S. Census Bureau and the National Association of Home Builders. A look at the construction methods used to build this house shows that it is within reach of most experienced builders. But it is hardly average.

A PERFECT FIT. Surrounded by a variety of mostly traditional home styles, this barn-inspired exterior blends right in. The front porch splits the elevation and softens the transition from grade to the raised first floor. A wood trellis wraps the house to shade both the front porch and the south-facing first-floor windows.

## KITCHEN APPLIANCES

**COOKTOP AND OVEN**
Thermador 30-in., Masterpiece Series

**RANGE HOOD**
Best Eclisse with recirculation kit

**DISHWASHER**
Thermador 24-in. panel-ready Topaz

**KITCHEN LIGHTING**
LED track lighting

**REFRIGERATOR**
Thermador 30-in. custom two-door with bottom freezer

**KITCHEN COUNTERS**
Stainless steel

## A HOUSE WITHIN REACH

Thanks to improvements to the way we build and the availability of more efficient heating, cooling, and other appliances, energy use per household is on the decline in America. However, when grid losses are considered, our homes are still responsible for 21% of total energy use in the United States, following industry and transportation, according to the U.S. Energy Information Administration.

The most recent data available from the Department of Energy is from 2018, and it shows that together, residential and commercial building are responsible for 12% of site-generated greenhouse gases. Electricity production is responsible for 27% of greenhouse-gas emissions, and homes use more of the electricity produced in the U.S. than any other sector.

Speaking about the work of ZED, Stephanie is quick to proclaim, "Energy motivates us!" She and Jordan describe their approach to energy efficiency as a three-step process. First, design and build the house to conserve as much energy as possible. The building envelope—foundation, floors, walls, and roof—is the main focus here. Second, design and install the most efficient mechanical systems needed to heat and cool the house and to maintain fresh and healthy indoor-air quality. Finally, add renewables. With photovoltaic (PV) costs often as low as $3 per watt installed and after incentives, Jordan advises clients to add all the PV they can afford.

At Jordan's recommendation, Kirsten and Joe installed a 5kw PV system on their home, which qualified them for a state rebate. Between conservation measures and renewables, this home is using about 73% less energy than the average code-built home. That puts net-zero energy easily within reach should Kirsten and Joe decide at any point to make an additional investment in PV.

## DURABILITY IS IN THE DETAILS

On the day of a full moon in October 2012, Superstorm Sandy struck the New Jersey shore. Nearly 350,000 homes were damaged or destroyed by the severe wind and by the state's second-highest recorded floods. In Margate, an island town within the bull's-eye of Sandy's landfall, the foundation for Kirsten and Joe's home recently had been poured. This home, like many others across the country, is in a risky area to build.

For extra flood protection, Stephanie and Jordan raised the foundation 4 ft. above grade, a foot higher than the building department required at the time. Going higher would have made it difficult to fit the two-story home into the neighborhood's overall height limitation for buildings. The raised foundation allows water to flood beneath the house and to drain via water vents. It's detailed as an unconditioned crawlspace.

The first floor is framed with I-joists and is air-sealed and insulated with a combination of rigid foam and water-based spray foam. The 2x6 stick-frame walls are filled with dense-pack cellulose. The roof is framed with 12-in. I-joists, also filled with cellulose. Zip System sheathing provides the air barrier for most of the building.

The entire exterior—walls and roof—is covered with 4 in. of rigid polyisocyanurate foam. To Jordan, this approach to insulating the envelope is about durability as well as efficiency. "Exterior insulation keeps the wood framing warm and dry over the life of the house," he says. "If moisture gets into the wall cavity, it can dry to the inside because there is no interior vapor barrier."

Though some American manufacturers now offer triple-glazed, high-performance windows, ZED prefers European products—in this case, from Schüco. Jordan says that they are more cost-effective than the domestic offerings and have a modern style that many homeowners are looking for. Beyond thermal performance, these windows provide thermal comfort by keeping the mean radiant temperature, or the average temperature of all interior surfaces, consistent. Because they are not available in impact-resistant glass, the house has a fabric shutter system that can be deployed when strong winds are imminent.

Detailing the envelope and installing the windows were the trickiest parts of the project for Chris Alexander, the builder, who had not put up a high-performance house before this. "We had a lot of meetings and 60-something pages of plans," he says. "We usually have eight." About the permitting and inspection process, Chris reports, "The building inspector was thrilled that a house like this was being built around here."

# HOW MUCH DOES A BETTER HOME COST?

The answer, say Stephanie Horowitz and Jordan Goldman of ZeroEnergy Design (ZED), is typically about 5% to 8% more than a similarly finished code-built house. The home featured here cost $275 per sq. ft. of conditioned space, a premium of about 7.9%. This house is on the higher end of the price-increase continuum for a few reasons: It doesn't have the inexpensive space of a basement to lower the cost per square foot, and it's a bit smaller than the average new house. (All else being equal, larger houses have a lower cost per square foot.) A larger, fancier house with a basement typically will be at the 5% end of the range, sometimes even lower. Also, the budget for a high-performance house is allocated differently from that of a more average house. For example, more money is spent on the building envelope, which here includes European windows and doors.

The result of such spending is that the house requires a much smaller heating and cooling system.

There is a return on investment in the form of significantly lower utility bills. The ZED team estimates a payback period of nine to 14 years, depending on future energy costs. Yet Stephanie says, "We do not try to justify the improvements we make, relative to code construction, on an economic basis. There are too many benefits that cannot be monetized, such as thermal comfort, altruism, resilience, durability, and sound attenuation."

In one 12-month period, this house used $1,310 worth of electricity (7080kwh). By Jordan's calculations, a code-compliant house would have used $4,800 worth of gas and electricity (assuming gas heat and hot water for the code-built house). So this house operated with a 73% reduction in utility bills, almost $3,500 in annual savings.

**HERE'S HOW STEPHANIE AND JORDAN ARRIVED AT THE 7.9% INCREASE.**

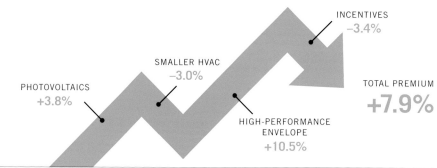

INCENTIVES
−3.4%

SMALLER HVAC
−3.0%

PHOTOVOLTAICS
+3.8%

TOTAL PREMIUM
+7.9%

HIGH-PERFORMANCE
ENVELOPE
+10.5%

**HERE'S WHERE THE HOUSE IS USING ITS ENERGY OVER THE COURSE OF A YEAR.**

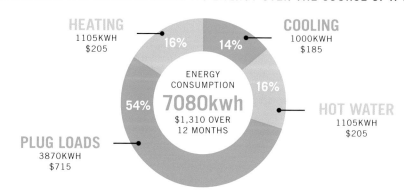

HEATING
1105KWH
$205

COOLING
1000KWH
$185

16%  14%

ENERGY
CONSUMPTION
**7080kwh**
$1,310 OVER
12 MONTHS

16%

HOT WATER
1105KWH
$205

54%

PLUG LOADS
3870KWH
$715

## EVERYTHING IS INEXTRICABLY LINKED

Not only does it make sense to use electric mechanicals and appliances in a home that produces electricity on its roof, but burning fossil fuels on-site is contrary to another of ZED's ethics: to provide healthy indoor air for clients. Combustion appliances are on the EPA's list of indoor pollutants, and a significant factor in poor indoor-air quality, according to the agency, is inadequate ventilation.

"It's all inextricably linked," says Stephanie. "When you address air infiltration, for example, you're addressing energy efficiency, thermal comfort, and indoor-air quality." In this case, ZED's approach to airflow was to build an extremely tight house (0.47 ACH50) and to provide plenty of fresh air with a Venmar energy-recovery ventilator and a balanced ventilation system. Fresh air is continuously supplied to bedrooms and living spaces. Stale air is continually exhausted from the kitchen and baths, each of which has a boost switch to make sure that enough air is being exhausted when the rooms are in use.

Electric heating and cooling are supplied by a Mitsubishi minisplit heat pump. The house has a heat-pump water heater and an induction cooktop as well. The electric mechanicals and appliances don't introduce any pollutants to the house, nor do any of the zero-VOC adhesives, surfaces, finishes, and furniture. These efforts earned the EPA's Indoor airPLUS certification for the house.

Just as the systems of a house are inseparable, so are our national infrastructure and resources. The looming water crisis and what we can do about it in our homes is a fitting example. According to the U.S. Geological Survey, the average family of four uses between 320 gal. and 400 gal. of water a day in their home. Production of electricity, however, is the largest consumer of freshwater world-

## FIT FOR A FAMILY

Open plans have been the trend for many years. But too open is sometimes too much. Here, the entry is separated from the living areas and designed for function, as it serves as the family's main path into the house. While the kitchen and living room are open to one another, a multipurpose room on the first floor has pocket doors that can be closed for privacy.

**SPECS**

**Bedrooms:** 4, plus multipurpose room

**Bathrooms:** 3

**Size:** 2,600 sq. ft.

**Walls:** R-44

**Roof:** R-68

**Windows:** U-factor, 0.13; SHGC, 0.35

**Location:** Margate, N.J.

**Architect:** ZeroEnergy Design, zeroenergy.com

**Builder:** Chris Alexander, C. Alexander Building & Maintenance Co., calexanderllc.com

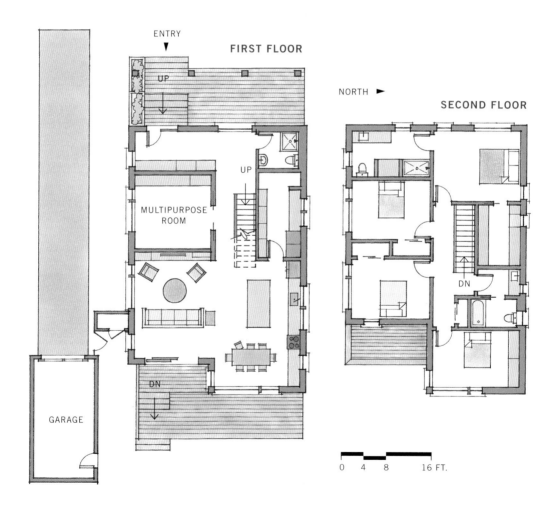

ENTRY

FIRST FLOOR

UP

NORTH ▶

SECOND FLOOR

UP

MULTIPURPOSE ROOM

DN

GARAGE

DN

0    4    8        16 FT.

wide. Kirsten and Joe's home conserves water first by producing its own electricity. But it also collects rainwater from the roof for landscape irrigation and has only water-efficient fixtures and appliances inside.

## AVERAGE SIZE BUT HARDLY AVERAGE

Kirsten and Joe had been living in an uninsulated, split-level "money pit" on this property before they found ZED and decided to build a new home. Though they could have put a bigger house on the property, they were committed to building only what they needed. Kirsten had kept an idea file and knew she would like a "modern barn" aesthetic outside with a modern interior.

The home's orientation along the northern side of the lot maximizes solar gain during the winter, and the driveway acts as a buffer between Kirsten and Joe's home and a neighboring home. Cost-saving is inherent to the home's simple shape. Splitting the elevation between grade and the first floor with the deck minimizes the visual impact of raising the house and means no handrail is needed. The planters and trellis add a clean modern edge. In a neighborhood with no prevailing architectural style, the exterior is unlikely to offend anyone's design sensibilities.

Stephanie's challenge was to design an interior that reflects the way Kirsten, Joe, and their three children would live in the house. The front entry, for example, was an important consideration in a home near the beach with street parking. Instead of opening into the great room or to a long view, which is so common today, the front entry opens to a bench and built-in storage cabinets. A full bathroom is only steps away.

The inside of the house is clean and modern. There is minimal trim, the stairs are open and sparse, the finishes are light in color, and generous storage keeps each room uncluttered. Natural wood was used for the floors and stairs, as well as an accent in the kitchen cabinetry. And plenty of sunlight warms the home literally and in that blissful-Sunday-morning way.

Since the house was built, Margate has adopted the 2018 International Residential Code (IRC). In terms of energy performance and indoor-air quality, this home still far exceeds it. In the wake of Superstorm Sandy, some resiliency provisions, such as the height to which a home must be elevated above grade, have been increased by the township.

Yet legislation is unlikely to be the force that makes a significant impact on how we build. The International Code Council (ICC) updates the nation's most commonly used residential codes every three years, but it often takes a number of years before the updates are adopted. California has an ambitious goal that all new homes built in the state will achieve net-zero energy use, but critics fear that simply adding renewable energy to average houses misses the most important aspect of high-performance homes: conservation.

With the dire forecast of climate change and more severe weather patterns predicted for the future, the likelihood of continued unpredictable fuel prices, and the knowledge and technology to build smarter and better than average, it's time to demand more of our homes. It's time to build more houses like this—houses that prove how easy it is to outperform the average.

# A NEW OLD FARMHOUSE

A new farm-house features historically inspired details executed with low-maintenance materials

BY IAN McDONALD

IN THE 1840S, GABRIEL CROOK, A LOCAL CARPENTER, builder, and architect, designed and built four Greek Revival houses on Shelter Island, N.Y. In the tradition of the time, all the materials used in their construction were milled or manufactured locally and transported by boat from Long Island and New England. Crook left the island in 1849 to seek fortune in California's gold rush, but his houses remain and continue to inspire those who live and visit here (see the sidebar on p. 104). As a resident of Shelter Island, I once had the great opportunity to study one of the four Crook houses in detail. I planned one day to build myself a house that would be inspired by his work.

When new clients approached me to design their new house, they were under contract to purchase 2.6 acres that backed up against Sylvester Manor, the original island homestead dating to 1652. The property also edged Dering Harbor, a village with approximately 30 formal, white-painted colonial houses. Like many who decide to build on this island, they were looking for a traditional design that would fit the regional architecture. However, instead of a historical reproduction, they wanted the house to have a contemporary quality and be easy to manage and maintain. The house also had to be large enough to accommodate visits from their extended family.

In one of our early meetings, I showed the clients a sketch of the Greek Revival farmhouse I was planning to build for myself, based on my study of Crook's house. They were instantly drawn to it. So began the challenge of constructing a new house that looked old to complement a modern way of living and a rich island history.

## MY INTERPRETATION OF A PATTERN-BOOK STYLE

As the Greek Revival style made its way from cities to the countryside through the use of pattern books, the details were often simplified or changed as the result of builder interpretation and the availability of local building materials. Just as the old carpenters interpreted details from pattern books, I chose to interpret the details of the old house that I had studied. Looking at a house that is 160 years old, you can't always tell whether all the details are original to the structure or if they were replaced or altered in the course of its history.

During my study of the Crook original, I took careful measurements of the various elements, down to the size of the different dentils. I made adjustments, but the old house served as my pattern throughout the process. By working through its details, I believe that the original spirit of the old house has been realized in this new structure.

# A PATTERN FOR DURABLE EXTERIOR DETAILS

## GREEK EAVES

The eave is composed of primary and secondary soffits and friezes to give an additional level of detail and to ease the dentil assembly. The secondary soffit and frieze were sized in place and then assembled indoors before being installed. The smaller, secondary dentils were varied in width so that a larger dentil would land on each corner perfectly.

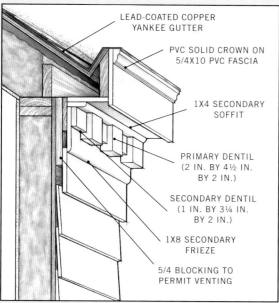

LEAD-COATED COPPER YANKEE GUTTER

PVC SOLID CROWN ON 5/4X10 PVC FASCIA

1X4 SECONDARY SOFFIT

PRIMARY DENTIL (2 IN. BY 4½ IN. BY 2 IN.)

SECONDARY DENTIL (1 IN. BY 3¼ IN. BY 2 IN.)

1X8 SECONDARY FRIEZE

5/4 BLOCKING TO PERMIT VENTING

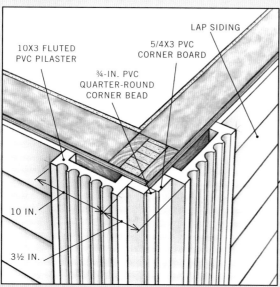

10X3 FLUTED PVC PILASTER

¾-IN. PVC QUARTER-ROUND CORNER BEAD

LAP SIDING

5/4X3 PVC CORNER BOARD

10 IN.

3½ IN.

## CUSTOM CORNERS

Ten-in. pilasters were specified for the corners so that their capitals would be of a similar proportion to the 12-in. column capitals supporting the porch roof. The pilasters were located so that their capitals would return fully on the corner boards.

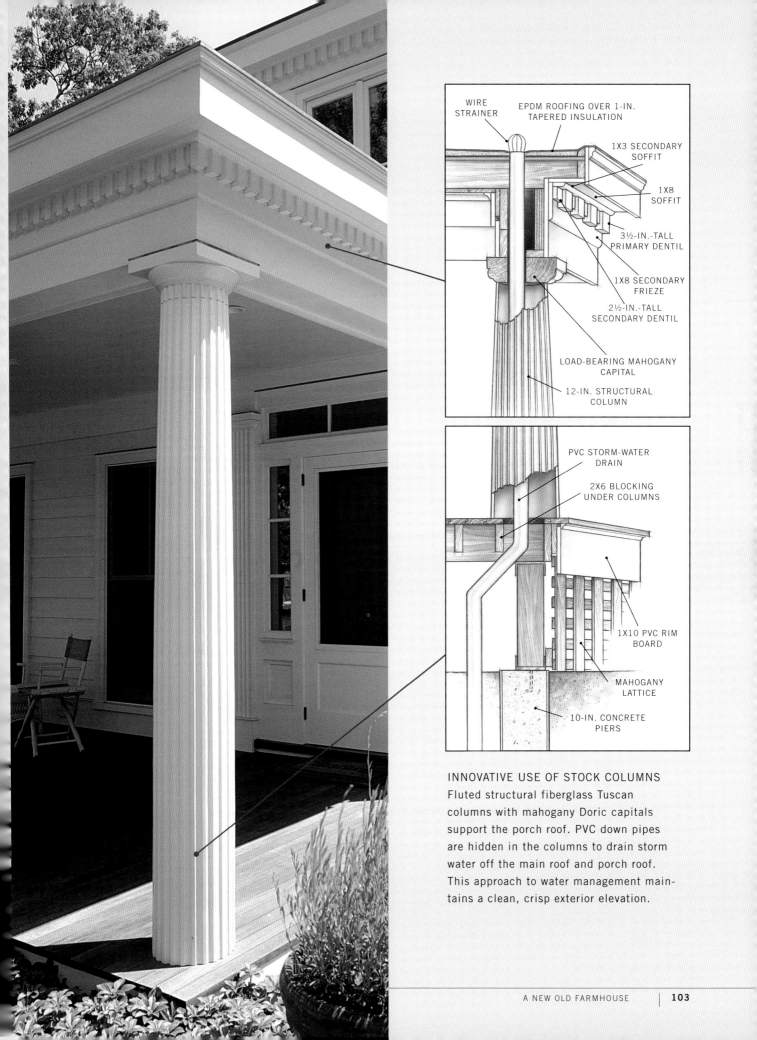

WIRE STRAINER

EPDM ROOFING OVER 1-IN. TAPERED INSULATION

1X3 SECONDARY SOFFIT

1X8 SOFFIT

3½-IN.-TALL PRIMARY DENTIL

1X8 SECONDARY FRIEZE

2½-IN.-TALL SECONDARY DENTIL

LOAD-BEARING MAHOGANY CAPITAL

12-IN. STRUCTURAL COLUMN

PVC STORM-WATER DRAIN

2X6 BLOCKING UNDER COLUMNS

1X10 PVC RIM BOARD

MAHOGANY LATTICE

10-IN. CONCRETE PIERS

## INNOVATIVE USE OF STOCK COLUMNS

Fluted structural fiberglass Tuscan columns with mahogany Doric capitals support the porch roof. PVC down pipes are hidden in the columns to drain storm water off the main roof and porch roof. This approach to water management maintains a clean, crisp exterior elevation.

# THE CROOK COLLECTION

The four Greek Revival homes built by Gabriel Crook still stand on Shelter Island, including the one that served, in many ways, as the pattern for this new home (photo below left).

## HOUSE SHAPE SUGGESTS A LONG HISTORY

After developing a list of requirements with my clients, I typically go through a few rounds of hand-drawn sketches that try to accommodate and organize all their requests. Instead of placing all these spaces or functions in a simple one- or two-layer box, I try to break them apart. This way, the house is allowed to develop additions or wings. The end result is often a house that appears to have been added on to over many years: a new house with historic charm.

On this project, the site constraints called for a long, narrow house and garage perpendicular to the harbor. Basing the house on the 22-ft.-wide Crook model, I developed a plan that used two of his houses like bookends connected by a "bridge" section in the middle. The powder room, guest bedrooms and their bathrooms, staircases, and laundry went in the rear bookend, which opened the entire first floor in the front section. The design allowed expansive harbor views from the living and dining room, the kitchen, and the three-season porch. The garage became a barnlike detached structure that allowed us to create an outdoor room between the two buildings.

## A FARMHOUSE FACADE THAT IS SURE TO LAST

All around Shelter Island and the eastern end of Long Island stand simple farmhouses that are utilitarian in size, layout, and detail. Almost all have a covered porch, and on many, the porch extends across the entire front of the house. The fronts of the houses have symmetrically placed 2-over-2 double-hung windows on the first floor, and smaller 2-over-2 double-hung windows on the second.

Crook's house shared many of these same attributes but had been adorned with elements common to the Greek Revival style: dentiled friezes, door-size 2-over-2 double-hung units made to look like French casement windows, fluted columns, an entry door wrapped in fluted trim, and corner boards made to look like fluted pilasters.

Unlike the carpenters of the past, we were able to source materials that are less likely to rot. Most of the exterior trim—frieze boards, fascia, crown, dentils, water tables, pilasters, and corner boards—are made of cellular PVC. The columns are made of structural fiberglass, and the siding is made of fiber cement. I chose Marvin windows with wood frames and metal-clad sashes for this house. The

AN ORNAMENTAL ENTRY WITH MULTI-PURPOSE DETAILS. A paneled door closely mirroring that in the Crook house opens onto the main living space. Above a Rumford fireplace, a mantel from Decorators Supply of Chicago features egg-and-dart trim details and fits the character of the space, while a built-in bookcase also serves as a buffet when entertaining guests and as a chase to hide unsightly HVAC supply and return grilles.

AN OPEN KITCHEN CREATES A MODERN FEEL. A commanding island with a 2-in.-thick statuary top and a 2¼-in.-thick white-oak top runs parallel to a wall of upper and lower cabinets with honed absolute-black granite countertops. The kitchen opens onto a screened porch to the north and into the living and dining room to the west.

## A PLAN FOR A CONTEMPORARY INTERIOR

The typical 1840s farmhouse, such as the Crook house, had a small footprint: roughly 22 ft. wide by 26 ft. deep with numerous small rooms. By comparison, this design has a living room equivalent to the entire Crook first floor, including the bay window.

The new floor plan puts two Crook-style houses to use and bridges the gap between them with a kitchen on the first floor and an office on the second floor.

**SPECS**

**Bedrooms:** 6
**Bathrooms:** 5½
**Size:** 2,755 sq. ft. (house);
695 sq. ft. (garage)
**Cost:** $349 per sq. ft.
**Completed:** 2010
**Location:** Shelter Island, N.Y.
**Architect:** Ian McDonald
**Builder:** Brett Poleshuk

**FIRST FLOOR**

NORTH ▶

**SECOND FLOOR**

0 2 4  8 FT.

clad sashes better protect the operational components of the windows, and only the flat work, jambs, and casings required painting.

On Shelter Island, we are required to design for a 120-mph three-second wind gust. We must either install window sashes with hurricane-rated glass or provide $1/2$-in. plywood panels that can be screwed to the framing beneath the exterior window casings in the event of a storm. For cost reasons, most homeowners opt for the plywood panels. With their wood frames and casings, the window units we used are much easier to repair after they have been screwed through than windows with aluminum-clad casings.

## APPROPRIATELY DETAILING A CONTEMPORARY INTERIOR

The homeowners had lived previously in a formal colonial house with a separate entry, living and dining room, library, and kitchen, and now wanted an open floor plan. The less formal approach to the layout was also more in tune with the rural character of the area.

Instead of the formal rooms, I designed a living room that has four areas: an entry, a seating area, a reading nook, and a dining area. The kitchen, which is located in the "bridge," is set apart from the other living spaces by a large cased opening. This gives it a modern open feel while maintaining the traditional notion of separation. The cased opening and a wall containing several windows looking onto a pond created some significant storage challenges.

To resolve this, I designed an island that houses the sink, the dishwasher, and a recycling bin on one side and that functions as a table on the other. I placed the island 4 ft. from the range to allow movement to and from the back of the house. The south wall is sectionalized into functions. The area closest to the living room holds wine glasses and a small bar sink. The range, microwave, and cooking gear are in the middle section. Close to the rear door and refrigerator is a pantry section with floor-to-ceiling storage.

## THE ARCHITECT/BUILDER RELATIONSHIP

On any project, collaboration is key. I found contractor Brett Poleshuk, with whom I had not previously worked, to be just as interested in the idiosyncrasies of the house as I. His willingness to explore unfamiliar details by reviewing pattern books, surfing online, or examining local houses enabled him to propose creative ways to achieve the sought-after aesthetic.

Since the house's completion in 2010, I repeatedly get asked two questions: "Was this a difficult renovation?" and "When was the original house constructed?" I can think of no better accolade for our efforts.

# SHAKER SIMPLICITY

This new zero-energy home captures the spirit of the Shakers with elegant details and a straight-forward plan

BY BRIAN PONTOLILO

AT ITS BEST, RESIDENTIAL DESIGN HAS LITTLE TO DO with the buildings themselves and everything to do with how we experience them. Some of us understand the details that make a house special—skillful use of views and light, trim and proportions, finishes and colors. But for most of us, it's the feeling of "home" that matters—that we feel welcome when we enter and that we feel at ease as our life unfolds within the building's embrace. It was likely this living experience that Rafe Churchill's clients were pointing to when they showed up to their first meeting with a children's book titled *One Morning in Maine* and asked Rafe to design and build a home inspired by it.

The book is about a young girl losing her first tooth, but in its first few pages are illustrations of a quaint home. These simple drawings led Rafe to study and pull from the modest style of Shaker architecture for this project. Yet it's not the details, colors, or floor plan that make this farmhouse worthy of celebration. Rather, it's the subtlety with which the house succeeds as a humble backdrop for family life. And it's also the fact that within this home that captures the qualities of an early American style, there hides a high-performance building assembly with a high-tech mechanical system that produces nearly all the energy the home needs.

## GETTING NEW/OLD RIGHT

The homes that Rafe Churchill designs and builds demonstrate his mastery of the new/old aesthetic, which he has earned through decades of experience as a remodeler in the historic towns of southern New England. Though he has drawn from the Shaker style before, he says that the owners of his house were his first clients "really interested in the Shaker experience—not only simple style, but simple living."

To research Shaker life and Shaker architecture, Rafe visited the Hancock Shaker Village in Pittsfield, Mass. (see the sidebar on p. 115). There, among other things, Rafe found inspiration for the first detail that catches your attention about this home: its color. Visible from the country road a few hundred yards across a wildflower meadow, the golden siding and crisp gable are the first suggestion that something special awaits at the end of the property's long gravel drive. A large meadow, a rustic barn, a working vegetable garden, and a utilitarian woodshed create an authentic farmstead experience as you approach the house.

At a closer look, the striking color seen from the street is balanced by the simple exterior details. The cedar clapboards, flat window and door casings, corner and frieze boards, and simple cornice profile are all painted the same color as the siding. Hung from the head casing with

THE HEIGHT ADVANTAGE.
Perhaps uncommon in an
early American house, the
tall 9-ft. ceilings allow these
built-ins to come to life. The
fireplace and hearth carry
the brick color and texture
of the foundation and mudroom into the house.

SPACE TO DINE. The large dining room easily could
accommodate built-ins or extra furniture, but the house
was designed for simple living, and the interior design
follows suit. The naturally finished pine floors maintain
the authentic farmhouse charm.

## A CENTRAL HALL AND ROOM TO BREATHE

Though the home is not small, everything about it, including the floor plan, is modest and understated. The central hallways and stair provide circulation to the four living spaces on the first floor and to the four bedrooms on the second floor. Occupying a corner of the home, each room has windows on two walls for views and cross ventilation. The mudroom annex offers a functional family entrance and suggests an addition, which would have been likely on an early American home.

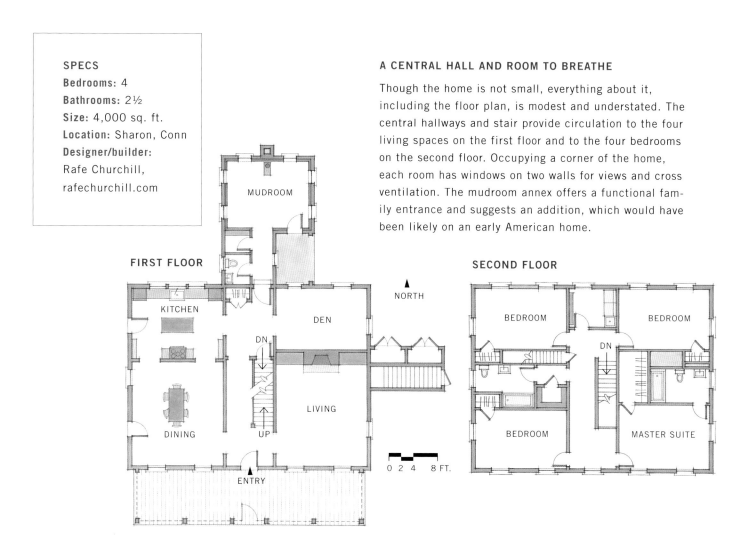

**FIRST FLOOR**

MUDROOM

KITCHEN

DEN

DN

LIVING

DINING

UP

ENTRY

NORTH

0 2 4 8 FT.

**SECOND FLOOR**

BEDROOM

BEDROOM

DN

BEDROOM

MASTER SUITE

visible clips, wooden screens provide the look of 100-year-old storms over the home's traditionally styled double-hung windows. The metal roof and south-facing solar panels are the only exterior elements that suggest a modern house.

Inside the home, the interplay of simple trim and cabinetry, historic details, and bold colors continues. The walls and ceilings are finished with natural plaster and polished to reveal a handcrafted texture. The southern-pine floors downstairs have a clear, low-sheen, water-based finish. Rafe says that this finish—Naturale from Bona—is as close as you can get to an unfinished look. The floors upstairs are painted gloss white. The trim is unremarkable in profile—just basic beaded baseboard and casings and a simple cove crown. The cabinetry is also quite modest, with inset flat-panel doors and

drawer fronts. These elements stand out, however, with a total of 18 paint colors used throughout the interior.

For an authentic look and experience inside the house, Rafe used some reclaimed materials, including the bathroom sinks, and chose old-fashioned pull-string lights for the closets. He also located outlets in the baseboards, suggesting that electricity was not original to the house. For their part, the homeowners followed through with appropriate furniture and minimal decoration. Even a functional rotary telephone hangs on the wall outside the kitchen.

"Most people don't know how to do simple," said Rafe. "They overcomplicate things. These clients stayed true to their vision."

**ABOVE:** HALLMARK HALLWAY. The hallway's peg rail is classic Shaker style, as are the delicate, turned stairway balusters and newel. Fixtures from PW Vintage Lighting and a rotary phone add authentic style.

**LEFT:** A COLORFUL COUNTRY KITCHEN. The unadorned Shaker-style cabinetry in the kitchen is brought to life with a lively color and a combination of countertops: black granite flanking the range and natural maple on the island. Open shelves on the wall add to the country appeal.

## A WARM AND QUIET BUILDING

In today's world of superinsulated slabs, double-stud walls, and the race to build the tightest high-performance home, the same may be true: We could be overcomplicating things. Rafe didn't do any energy modeling for this house or even have a blower-door test performed during construction. He drew from his experience and kept the building assembly as straightforward as possible. The floors are framed with I-joists, the walls with structural insulated panels (SIPs), and the roof with attic trusses.

Rafe's preference for SIP walls has to do with their thermal performance. The 8-in.-thick SIP walls in this house offer R-28 expanded polystyrene insulation with minimal thermal bridging and without the need for exterior foam or a complicated wall assembly. The seams are air-sealed before being covered by felt. The siding is installed over furring strips.

SUBTLE AND SOPHISTICATED. The exterior colors and details are simple and elegant: cedar siding and trim, four-panel mahogany doors, and double-hung windows painted with an accent color. Brick veneer dresses up the foundation and the porch piers. The most sophisticated detail is perhaps the subtlest: A bevel at the top of the skirt matches the pitch of the siding.

THE PERFECT PORCH. No country home is complete without a front porch. Here, the flooring is reclaimed ipé. The ceiling is painted a traditional blue.

The trusses create usable attic space for storage and mechanicals and were easily insulated to R-40 with open-cell spray polyurethane foam. The roof was sheathed and covered with felt, furred out with strapping to create a vent space, and sheathed again before the roofers applied metal-roof underlayment and standing-seam panels.

The basement is insulated to R-20 with rigid foam on both sides of the concrete walls. The floor assemblies and all interior walls are insulated with recycled denim, a sound-deadening measure.

The house took nine months to build, and Rafe says that getting a dry, heatable structure up quickly is part of making any build go smoothly. Building with these structural components lends a big hand to that effort.

## THE MECHANICALS ARE OUT OF SIGHT

The common entrance to this house is not the front door, but a back entry that opens into a mud-room. The open-stud walls, exposed rafters, brick floor, and woodstove in this mudroom conjure a past day of farm chores and wood heating. The real heating system is nowhere in sight in the mud-room, however, or anywhere else in the house.

The first and second floors have hydronic, in-floor radiant heat. The absence of baseboard heaters helps to maintain the home's simplicity. A visit to the basement, though, reveals a sophisti-cated mechanical system.

Two geothermal heat pumps, each paired with a hot-water storage tank, provide both the radiant heat and the home's potable hot water. Geother-mal heating also means that there is no boiler or furnace burning fossil fuels on-site or disturbing the home's restful atmosphere.

Instead of air-conditioning, the home stays cool in the summer with a powerful whole-house fan in the attic and positive cross ventilation in all rooms. For fresh air, there are heat-recovery ventilators to serve each floor. The bath fans are also ducted through this fresh-air supply, and each floor has a dedicated humidifier to keep humidity levels up during winter. The kitchen's range hood has a ded-icated makeup-air supply that is preheated by an in-line electric coil.

This all-electric system is powered by a 10kw net-metered solar array. The pool's heating is the only draw not being covered by on-site energy production.

The home also has two plumbing systems. The first is a conventional system for potable water, which is supplied by a well. The second is a rain-water system that provides water for the toilets, irrigation, and the pool.

## A HOME BUILT TO LAST

The Shakers' values of simplicity and their contribu-tions to architecture, construction, and craft were inspired by the community's beliefs. The care with which they built was an expression of those beliefs. Perhaps this is why their buildings still stand and their furniture is still replicated. Rafe shares these values in many ways.

"The most sustainable thing we can do," he says, "is build durable homes and maintain them well." Rafe believes first and foremost in using qual-ity materials and hiring quality craftspeople. "A house has to be built well," he explains, "no matter what materials you use—or you'll be building it over again soon."

With that intention, this new home is sure to make a great old house someday.

The meetinghouse at the Hancock Shaker Museum

The brethren's shop at the Hancock Shaker Museum

## BUILDING WITH THE CARE OF PRAYER

The Shakers are a religious order that originated in England in the 1700s. On August 6, 1774, Mother Ann Lee—a prominent Shaker leader—and a small group of followers landed in New York City and soon moved north to a swampy parcel of land near Albany. Here, the first Shaker settlement began to take shape. By 1793, there were nearly a dozen Shaker settlements throughout New England. It was on these settlements that the Shaker style emerged.

At the heart of these communities was the meetinghouse, often the first building in a new Shaker village. Typically wood-framed, white-clapboard buildings with gambrel roofs and abundant double-hung windows, most meetinghouses had a large, open first floor for worship and dance. The second floor was divided into separate residences for men and women. The minimalism of these buildings was born of the Shaker ideal of purposeful simplicity but also out of necessity, as a fledgling community often had limited resources.

"If Shaker buildings seem familiar to us," says Shawn Hartley Hancock of the Hancock Shaker Museum in Pittsfield, Mass., "it's because their communities grew up around the existing homes and farms of the first converts, reflecting the timber-frame construction, gambrel roofs, and clapboard siding of Anglo-Dutch architecture."

As the communities grew, the original elements of design were largely maintained. Some details did become more interesting: More colors were used, and brick and stone were sometimes substituted for the traditional wood exteriors. Other details were simplified further: Straightforward gables often replaced the original gambrel roofs. Interiors remained strictly functional, as did their furnishings.

"Shaker buildings reflect impressive forethought," says Hancock. "Barrel roof designs were used to shed snow and rain. Deep plaster cove cornices minimized heat loss through the attic. For ease of maintenance, gable roofs over exterior doors often had no supports. The ubiquitous Shaker built-in cupboards and peg rails allowed rooms to be cleaned and organized easily, while interior windows allowed light deep into large rooms."

Shakers dedicated their life to worship. They approached their work as a spiritual act. Putting the care of prayer into all that they did explains the high quality and durability of Shaker buildings, furniture, and goods.

For more information, visit hancockshakervillage.org.

# COLD-CLIMATE FARM

A Maine architect designs Michigan's first certified Passive House to be rooted in tradition

BY MATT O'MALIA

I PRACTICE ARCHITECTURE IN MID-COAST MAINE, a cold area that can experience some of the country's most beautiful and most brutal weather. This undoubtedly has had an impact on my approach to design. As an architect, I believe I'm composing a long-term picture of resource consumption, durability, and comfort in the homes I help to create. As a result, I feel it's my responsibility to be as mindful about the implications of my designs as possible. With this idea at the core of my practice, I use the Passive House performance standard when I can to help achieve what we at my firm believe to be a healthy, comfortable, and highly sustainable home throughout its life span. Over the years, more and more people across the country have found value in the very same logic.

It was not a complete surprise when my good friend Michael Klinger—a certified Passive House consultant, a builder, and the owner of Energy Wise Homes in Michigan—called me to pitch a low-energy project in the rural town of Holly. He had already been working with clients Maura and Kurt, who were passionate about building a certified Passive House on their rolling property.

While Michigan and Maine are a considerable distance apart, both are located in the northern tier of the country, and their climates are very similar. I felt that the designs we'd been working on over the years here in Maine would be ideally suited to the home Maura and Kurt hoped to build.

Early on, we established a goal to work within the local farmhouse style. Our early design meetings led to a plan that would strike a balance between design objectives and budget, while ensuring the construction of a home that was 90% more efficient than the average American house.

ENERGY SMART. This transitional farmhouse in rural Michigan successfully captures the comforts of traditional design in a cutting-edge, high-performance home.

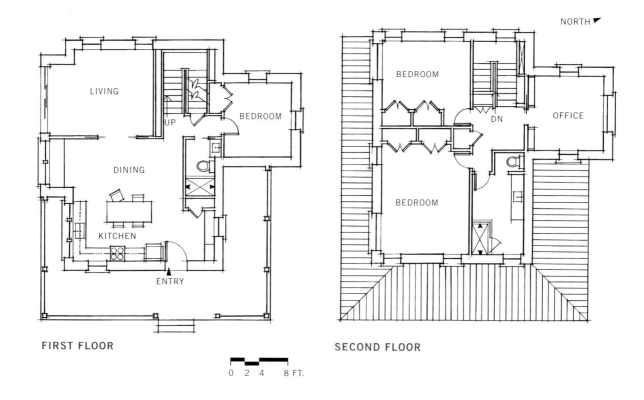

FIRST FLOOR

SECOND FLOOR

NORTH ▼

LIVING

UP

BEDROOM

DINING

KITCHEN

ENTRY

BEDROOM

DN

OFFICE

BEDROOM

0 2 4 8 FT.

SPECS

**Bedrooms:** 3, plus office

**Bathrooms:** 2

**Size:** 2,440 sq. ft.

**Location:** Holly, Mich.

**Architects:** Matt O'Malia and Riley Pratt, GO Logic, gologic.us

**Builder:** Michael Klinger, Energy Wise Homes, Inc.

# A FARMHOUSE IN TRANSITION

The design of this home is based on the hallmarks of the farmhouse style. Instead of a traditional interpretation, however, the homeowners wanted a slightly more contemporary home. Contemporary details were driven by the design elements associated with building a high-performance home.

1 A simple gable roof is the most energy-efficient form to use, and it helps to establish the home's traditional look.

2 Standing-seam metal roofing offers durability and longevity; moreover, it connects the home to its rural region, which is dotted with farms and outbuildings of similar proportion and detail.

3 A sweeping front porch helps define the style as a quintessential farmhouse, and its roof pitch is adjusted for optimum solar gain through south-facing windows.

4 Low-maintenance, fiber-cement lap siding, painted Sherwin-Williams Indian Corn red, wraps the house and the barnlike detached garage.

5 Overscale, 2-over-2 triple-glazed windows by Kneer-Süd allow views and solar energy to penetrate deep into the living space and shift the home's style toward the contemporary.

6 Inset windows give the exterior walls visual depth and mass. The resulting shadowlines create punches of contrast and keep the unadorned elevations from looking bleak.

## A COLD-CLIMATE SOLUTION

Interest in Passive House has grown significantly over the past several years, and while there are still relatively few certified projects in this country, the standard has been met with homes built in California, Virginia, and a variety of places in between.

Passive House presents itself as being an appropriate building standard for almost all climates and locations. But we at our firm ask whether or not the added investment in the building shell demanded by Passive House is cost-effective in all climates.

We don't think it is; moreover, the cost-effectiveness of meeting the Passive House standard needs to be analyzed closely on a case-by-case basis. For example, in extremely cold climates, the levels of insulation needed to achieve Passive House certification are so great that it does not make practical sense to meet the standard. However, the basic approach to the construction of a Passive House—creating a highly insulated, air-sealed shell and integrating heat-recovery ventilation—makes perfect sense even if certification isn't achieved. Similarly, in a Southern climate, building a home to meet Passive House certification becomes less relevant because of the lack of a significant space-heating demand.

Despite our regionalized view of Passive House, meeting the standard has many benefits. Unlike

# A PASSIVE HOUSE, PIECE BY PIECE

### ROOF

1 $\frac{5}{8}$-in. roof sheathing

2 #30 felt paper

3 28 in. loose-fill cellulose

4 Vent baffles

5 $\frac{1}{2}$-in. ZIP System sheathing (air barrier)

6 Air-sealed rigid-foam blocking

### WALL

1 2x6 stud wall

2 Dense-pack cellulose

3 $\frac{1}{2}$-in. ZIP System sheathing (air barrier)

4 $11\frac{7}{8}$-in. I-joist Larsen truss

5 Dense-pack cellulose

6 $\frac{5}{8}$-in. fiberboard sheathing

7 Housewrap

8 1x furring strips

### FLOOR

1 2x sleeper

2 $1\frac{1}{2}$ in. concrete

### FOUNDATION

1 2x4 stud wall

2 Dense-pack cellulose

3 Continuous vapor/air barrier

4 ICF foundation wall

5 Waterproof membrane

6 6-in. EPS rigid foam

7 Parge coating

8 8-in. XPS rigid foam

LIGHT-FILLED LIVING. The main floor is arranged as an open living space, where the kitchen, dining room, and living room share access to daylight and views. All of the interior spaces are painted Sherwin-Williams Woodlawn Snow, a soft white that serves as a neutral backdrop for the owners' collected furnishings.

other green-building standards that require environmentally friendly design decisions based on a particular value system, the predictive nature of the Passive House modeling software allows designers to complete a cost-benefit analysis related to energy consumption and construction—and that's where we see its real value. When designing this home in Michigan, we were able to run different shell scenarios through the software and then assess what details had the most impact on energy usage and therefore on long-term energy costs. Without this predictive energy-modeling capability, there is no way to assess the actual value of, say, adding an additional 12 in. of insulation to the roof or walls.

## A PRACTICAL AND EFFICIENT SHELL

While there are a variety of ways to construct a Passive House, this certified Michigan project has a few details that are slightly different. First, the clients wanted a crawlspace. We had to rethink our foundation design to offer the extra functionality without incurring a significant energy penalty. Second, the contractor wanted to use an insulated-concrete-form (ICF) foundation and a Larsen-truss wall assembly. While not the typical detailing we use, this strategy is a common method of constructing highly insulated walls.

## SAVINGS IN SMALL MECHANICALS

All of our efforts in designing and building the shell of the home paid off when it came to choosing and sizing the mechanical systems. Because the shell is so tight, this home requires very small

A KITCHEN WITH A VIEW. Locally built quartersawn white-oak kitchen cabinets evoke an important sense of craftsmanship. Yet the design of the kitchen and adjacent dining space isn't intended to retain your focus on the interior at all. Upper cabinets have been replaced by a trio of casement windows, and a massive tilt-turn window unit in the dining area draws you out into the landscape that makes this property so exceptional.

inputs to maintain comfortable indoor temperatures. Heat-recovery ventilation, which provides a supply of fresh air with minimal heat loss, is the primary aspect of climate control. Supplemental heating and cooling is accomplished with ductless minisplits.

These mechanical systems are simple, efficient, and relatively inexpensive. Heating systems that are more typical, such as oil or gas boilers, would be oversize for a house like this.

Also, because these systems run on electricity, a photovoltaic system can quickly bring the home down to net zero. Though it wasn't included in the original construction of this home, a grid-tied 6480kw PV array that Maura and Kurt are now installing will completely satisfy their energy demands.

## PLACE-BASED DESIGN

Maura and Kurt have a deep personal commitment to their land, and they hope to restore it to its native condition. It was important to them to have a house that looked like it had always been there. The property, which has a farming history dating back to 1836, once had a farmhouse standing on it. The stone foundation of that house still pokes through the prairie grass on the eastern edge of the property.

The house is set on the crest of a small hill and is skewed to provide access to sunlight and views through its southern facade. We designed it to be compact to reduce its surface area and to align its proportions with houses typical of the surrounding area. The home doesn't dominate its setting, and it looks like it belongs.

# THE "PERFECT" TEXAS HOUSE

Putting the insulation outside of the walls opened up new design possibilities for this low-maintenance Texas home

BY MATT RISINGER AND ERIC RAUSER

WHEN GREG HEIDEL TOLD US THAT HE WANTED to "simplify the systems" of his life, he was speaking our language. Greg is a single guy who had recently purchased an empty lot in East Austin, Texas, an up-and-coming neighborhood. He wanted to build a new house that supported his lifestyle. Greg spends his time volunteering and saving money to donate to causes that are important to him, so he didn't want a house that would be expensive to heat and cool or one that would require a lot of time and money to maintain. We don't design many homes—we're building-science geeks, and we typically add our knowledge to other architects' designs. But Greg offered us the opportunity to both design and build his house, weaving proven building science into the plan from the get-go. We had the perfect approach in mind.

## OUTSULATION IS UNIVERSALLY SMART

Since we first read Joe Lstiburek's 2007 article, "The Perfect Wall," which describes an utterly simple yet radically unconventional building envelope, we've wanted to put it into practice in one of our projects. In the article, Joe outlines a wall assembly in which four control layers—one each for rain, air, vapor, and temperature—are installed outside the framing. Using this approach, the control layers protect the structure from water, vapor, and temperature swings, creating a more durable building. Though it is certainly still an option to put more insulation on the inside of a Perfect Wall, one of the main differences between this approach and the way most walls are built is that the primary thermal layer is on the outside. This assembly works in any climate; typically the only necessary adjustment is the thickness of the insulation. Another significant difference is that the purpose of the siding (and perhaps the way we should think of all siding) is only to protect the control layers from UV radiation.

The Perfect Wall is also the Perfect Roof and the Perfect Floor. Only slight tweaks are made when changing planes. Integrating the control layers as they transition from the slab to the walls and the walls to the roof is important. The layers must be continuous.

Nicknamed "the 500-year wall" because it is possibly the most durable way to build a house, the Perfect Wall approach met Greg's desire for low maintenance. And once we'd decided that the insulation would be installed outside of the structure, we were able to explore a unique design possibility that this approach offers.

FOR THE SAKE OF SIMPLICITY. A skillful execution of building-science principles and the quest for a simple, long-lasting home allows a unique detail to shine: the framing.

## THE PERFECT WALL IN PRACTICE

The Perfect Wall concept specifies four control layers, which building scientist Joe Lstiburek puts in this order of importance: rain, air, vapor, thermal. Here is how Matt and Eric built this house and executed each of these controls along the way.

The house is built on a pier-and-beam foundation over a vented crawlspace. The first-floor deck and inside of the rim joists are insulated from below with 1 in. of closed-cell spray foam, which acts as all the necessary controls for this location.

Before being sheathed with OSB for shear strength, the walls are covered with shiplapped pine, which will be exposed to the interior.

A peel-and-stick membrane from Carlisle acts as the air, rain, and vapor controls. Installed before the insulation, the membrane is protected from the sun and temperature fluctuations.

Staggered layers of rigid insulation (2-in. polyisocyanurate on the walls and 3-in. polyisocyanurate on the roof) act as the thermal barrier.

The walls and roof have a vented rainscreen assembly, providing ¾ in. of air space behind the siding and roofing, which protects the control layers from damaging UV light. The reflective metal siding, air gap, and foil-faced insulation also act as a radiant barrier to minimize radiant heat gain in the hot Texas climate.

There is no drywall to be found in this house. Everywhere you look, you see structure. Yet designing the home wasn't as simple as just leaving the structure exposed. There was a lot to consider and research before we even presented this idea to Greg.

First, we talked to the lumberyard. They agreed to allow us to cull the most attractive lumber for this house and we agreed to send what we didn't take from the stacks to other projects where the lumber would be more conventionally hidden in the walls and ceilings. Then we talked to the framers, who were immediately excited that their work would be visible. They helped us find solutions to many of the aesthetic challenges. For example, we didn't want a lot of toenailing, which often splits and splinters lumber. Above the window headers, where the cripples are commonly toenailed, the framers used a sill plate so the cripples could be through-nailed before being put into place. They also found ways to avoid the need for metal framing connectors and were extra precise with their nailing patterns.

Wanting the house to have a traditional quality, we didn't use any modern framing materials except for a couple of glulam beams where we needed long spans. The framers even used old-school cross-bracing between the floor joists, and we sheathed the house first with shiplapped pine, to be seen as the interior finish, followed by a layer of OSB to create a shear wall.

You might ask how we passed inspection without the fire protection that drywall offers. It turns out that even the building inspector liked the idea that the wall cavities would be exposed. Because the cavities are not continuous between floors, the inspector saw the open walls as advantageous for fighting a fire, should one occur.

## REPAIR AND REMODEL WITH EASE

If this house is going to last 500 years, Greg will likely not be the only homeowner, so it had better be easy to remodel. We found surprising opportunities for future remodeling while figuring out how to hide the electrical and plumbing runs.

All of the exposed wiring is metallic-sheathed cable and the outlets and switches are surface-mounted in metal boxes. This makes it easy to move and add outlets and switches. Most of the plumbing is hidden in closets or in the second-floor storage space behind the kneewall, which means that it is all easily accessible.

Both the plumber and electrician were helpful, creative, and neat with their work. In one particular case, the plumber took the time to bore a hole through the plates for a vent pipe that typically would have been notched into the front edge. This subtle difference, which left just a fraction of an inch of the face of the plate intact, made a big difference in appearance.

After living in the house for some time, Greg decided that he wanted to move the tub filler, which took us only a couple of hours since the supply lines are accessible without removing any finished surface. The only carpentry was to bore a new hole and repair the old hole in the bathroom's paneling. We assume that the kitchen, which is tucked into a bump-out, can be completely remodeled in just a day or two.

## A SIMPLE PLAN

The home's footprint was restricted by two things: protected old-growth pecan trees and the homeowner's goal of simplicity. Modeled after traditional Texas schoolhouses, the home is essentially a rectangle with only a small bump-out in the back for a little extra kitchen and mudroom space. The first floor is open, mostly public space with the option of a second bedroom. Upstairs is a master suite.

FIRST FLOOR

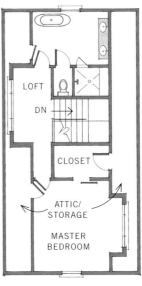

SECOND FLOOR

NORTH

0  2  4    8 FT.

SPECS

**Bedrooms:** 2

**Bathrooms:** 2

**Size:** 1,450 sq. ft.

**Location:** Austin, Texas

**Architect:** Eric Rauser, AIA, rauserdesign.com

**Builder:** Risinger & Co., risingerhomes.com

A BEAM AND A BUMP-OUT. The kitchen is nestled into a nook, defined by one of only two engineered beams in the house. In the roof behind the beam are skylights that bring sunlight to the work surfaces. The cabinetry is from IKEA.

## SEPARATE SYSTEMS

Our mechanical designer, Kristof Irwin, says that houses are like boats: the more leaks you have, the bigger bilge pump you need. This house has few leaks, so it didn't need a very big mechanical system. In fact, we used separate systems for heating and cooling, ventilation, and humidification.

The house has a single minisplit compressor with three interior units. To counter the stack effect, we installed a return register in the second-floor bathroom with a fan that sends warmer air back down to the first-floor utility room. An ERV replaces indoor air with fresh air from outside. Lastly, we installed a dehumidifier under the stairs, because in our humid climate it's important to be able to control temperature and relative humidity separately.

Because of their simplicity and accessibility, the mechanicals, like the plumbing and electrical systems, will be easy to update over time and as technology advances. That is one of the three keys to longevity that we applied to this project while using the most advanced building science available: Make it durable by protecting the structure, make it adaptable so it doesn't get torn apart or torn down, and keep it simple so it is easy to upgrade as we learn more about buildings and develop more efficient mechanical systems.

# A FARMHOUSE IN SUBURBIA

Timeless styling with a modern twist makes this new home stand out in a postwar New England neighborhood

BY ROB WOTZAK

TOM BURES AND LIESL SITTON REALIZED THAT their South Boston apartment was getting to be too small for their growing family at the same time that a house around the block from Tom's mother went on the market. The modest 1940s colonial wasn't quite what they were looking for, but they couldn't pass up the opportunity to be closer to family, so they bought it. At the time, the couple had only an inkling of the creative journey this purchase would take them on, but they knew they were determined to turn the place into a home they would love and live in for years to come.

Tom and Liesl's initial plan was to remodel and expand the small house to give the family everything they wanted in a home. After careful consideration, though, it seemed to make more sense to raze the existing house and start from scratch with a new build. Their goal was to build something different from the surrounding colonials and Capes, but at the same time, something that would fit in with the traditional style of the neighborhood.

## THE DESIGN CHALLENGE

While searching for inspiration, Tom and Liesl stumbled upon the design/build firm GO Logic in the book *Prefabulous + Almost Off the Grid*. They were initially drawn to GO Logic's minimalist take on New England architectural styles, but the firm's experience building sustainable, high-performance homes is what won them over in the end. Once Tom and Liesl got a feel for the talent and dedication of the GO Logic architects, they knew that designing the house would present the team with a fun and creative challenge. Jokingly, Tom told them to "design a house that would win an award," which is exactly what they did.

The design team's first priority was to figure out how the house would best fit into the traditional neighborhood. They chose clapboard siding, a standing-seam gable roof, and a tidy grid of four-lite windows to give the house a decidedly New England feel. But fitting an attached garage on the narrow lot without dominating the facade would prove to be a challenge. They went through many iterations, shifting the spaces of the first and second floors until they found a streamlined solution: an unusual tandem garage flanking the right side of the house, with the L-shaped second floor shifting over the top of the garage to make it tuck neatly under a cantilevered corner. This would allow the second floor over the main house to become more slender, which would ultimately bring more light into the space and make room for more windows in the master suite above the garage.

## MOVES TOWARD MODERN

The architects started with the form of a traditional Cape and two-car garage, and with three simple changes made it more modern and relevant for a contemporary family.

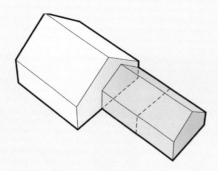

The starting form is a common Cape with a two-car garage.

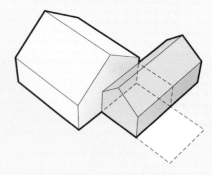

Turning the garage 90° minimizes its impact on the home's street-facing elevation. The garage still has two entrances, front and back.

HIDDEN IN PLAIN SIGHT. Recycled barn boards certainly stand out against the stark white clapboards on the rest of the house. But even though the contrasting siding catches your attention, you probably wouldn't spot the cleverly concealed garage door when it's closed.

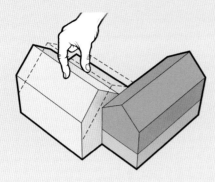

Adding a narrow second story over the main form and above the garage gives the home needed space and makes the roof pitch appropriate for the taller building.

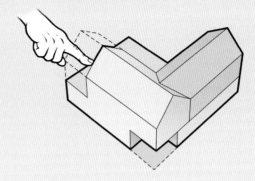

Shifting the second story toward the garage creates cover for the home's main entry and gives the house a more edgy, modern look with a big cantilever and single-story portions with a flat roof.

The garage has a front and rear entrance for practicality, and repurposed barn siding that wraps across the front door makes the front opening all but disappear when it's closed (photo facing page). Because the back door opens into the private backyard, it makes the rear half of the garage more flexible. In the warmer months, bikes and sports equipment take priority, but both of the family cars move inside for the winter.

Though one of the reasons for including the flat roof over the den and kitchen is to accommodate a green roof, the addition of vegetation and a rooftop deck was pushed off to a second phase of the project. The choice of a flat roof wasn't a given from the start—gable and shed roofs were also considered—but the flat roof fit best with the modern sensibilities of the overall design, and it dovetailed nicely with the distinctive jog in the house's facade.

## A HYBRID PLAN

For the interior details, Tom and Liesl brought in designer and former neighbor Anthony Lee. The designer, architects, and homeowners shared the same goal of pairing natural, honest materials with a layout that complements a casual lifestyle. They settled on a sort of hybrid floor plan—something between a traditional layout with separate rooms and a more contemporary open concept. This is most evident in the living and dining areas, where the two spaces are defined by bold accent walls and changes in ceiling height, but are really extensions of one large room. The rooms feel brighter and more spacious because of this, and no square footage is wasted on separate hallways.

In talking with GO Logic principal architect Matthew O'Malia, Tom and Liesl embraced the idea that bedrooms don't need to be big and complicated, and that they would get more bang for their buck investing time and money in multipurpose rooms like the kitchen and den. The couple was already on the right track with a purchase they made before the house was built: a salvaged set of cabinets that they were determined to work into the new kitchen.

Getting the most out of the den was merely a matter of designing it to meet several current and future needs. An adjacent bathroom allows it to double as a guest room. And because Tom and Liesl hope to be in the house for many years, they made sure it was private and accessible enough to possibly become the master bedroom someday.

## SIMPLE INSIDE

Though the house has an interesting form on the out-side, the floor plans are quite simple. The first floor is a square. The kitchen, dining room, family room, and den are well defined, yet there are no hallways to waste space. The second floor is an L-shape, with two basic bedrooms that share a bath, a multiuse space, and the master suite.

**SPECS**
**Bedrooms:** 4
**Bathrooms:** 3½
**Size:** 3,500 sq. ft.
**Cost:** $183 per sq. ft. (construction only)
**Completed:** 2015
**Location:** Wellesley, Mass.
**Architect:** GO Logic
**Builder:** Eco Structures

### FIRST FLOOR

1 Living
2 Dining
3 Kitchen
4 Den
5 Garage
6 Master suite
7 Walk-in closet
8 Multiuse room
9 Bedroom

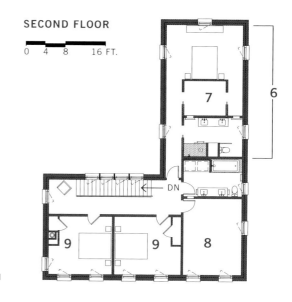

### SECOND FLOOR

0   4   8      16 FT.

MIXING OLD AND NEW. The wood feature wall and ceiling are built with salvaged red-oak flooring and define a warm, cozy seating area within the bright, modern living space.

A HINT OF DEFINITION. The dining room is defined by a fireplace wall clad with glazed bricks. More than just a beautiful centerpiece, the wall is tall enough to visually separate the dining and living spaces without disrupting the home's feeling of openness.

PLAYFUL USE OF COLOR. A red mosaic pattern in the tiled tub surround and matching red cabinet knobs liven up the kids' bathroom.

THE WARMTH OF WOOD. The large kitchen island is a magnet for a whole host of family activities. Colorful furniture and accessories placed throughout the house contrast with the muted paint scheme to make every room feel both soothing and full of energy.

The architects focused on integrating energy efficiency throughout the design process, basing their performance goals on the Passive House standard. Abundant triple-pane windows let in lots of light but keep precious heat from escaping. The superinsulated house gets heat and air conditioning from a Mitsubishi minisplit heat pump and fresh air from a Zehnder energy-recovery ventilator. All of these details paid off, judging from the annual heating costs of around $300.

The family says that the house is fabulous to live in. It's always comfortable and bright, and it fits the way they live. The most unanticipated thing about it is the attention it gets. Every person that comes to the house comments on how unique it is, and people passing through the neighborhood often slow down to get a better look—some even come up and ring the bell to ask about it.

# A SINGLE-STORY CABIN GROWS UP

Traditional materials and steeply sloped rooflines transform a boxy cabin into a modern farmhouse with a flexible floor plan that considers aging in place

BY MATTHEW SWETT

THIS PROJECT BEGAN WITH A BIRTHDAY PRESENT. Kathy, who attends my wife's yoga classes, learned that I'm an architect, and asked if she could gift some of my time to her husband, David, to help him design a small woodshop. Kathy, I soon discovered, is an avid weaver. She didn't know it at the time, but I had grown up in a woodshop making weaving looms with my parents. We were well matched.

A few hours consultation evolved into a full design for the woodshop. We worked well together and our collective attention turned next to their house. Kathy and David were nearing retirement and were considering transitioning from their home in Seattle to their property here on Whidbey Island. The existing cabin was a mere 800 sq. ft., and downsizing from their four-story Craftsman-style home was too much of a leap for the couple. However, they realized they could make it work with some thoughtful modifications.

## THE SITE STEERS DESIGN

The cabin was old—the first of its kind built at Bush Point. As such, it was well sited, high on the hill with sweeping views of the Salish Sea. Age added grace—over the years, the landscape had grown and the house had been enfolded in a mature grove of trees.

The building itself was small and oddly laid out. It lacked an entry; you arrived via French doors directly into the kitchen. The bathroom and bedrooms were tight and, in our rainy climate, the large, uncovered front deck was seldom used. The mechanical system was an afterthought, tacked on to the side of the building sometime in the last century. It needed some help.

Early in the design process, we agreed that stewarding the landscape was a high priority, so we decided to keep the footprint as close to the original as possible. We tried to retain as much of the existing structure as we could, but soon learned that was impractical. The existing ceilings were too low, the framing insubstantial, and the energy performance poor. The one bonus was that the foundation system had been upgraded in the recent past. Constrained on all sides, but with a solid foundation under us, we decided to marginally increase the footprint and add a second floor above. Ultimately, that meant nearly starting over on the existing foundation. Kathy and David had spent a considerable amount of time refurbishing the cabin's interior woodwork already (see sidebar on p. 145), so in the interest of preserving that resource and history, they carefully removed it for reinstallation in the new structure.

CREATING A CLASSIC LOOK. The cabin original to the site was cramped and squat, and its uncovered outdoor living space went unused much of the time. The remodeled house is everything the old structure was not. Designed in the farmhouse style, it has a covered porch, soaring gables, and an all-wood exterior that glows with inviting warmth. The wood's natural finish is complemented by the dark tones of the windows and roof, giving the exterior a simple yet striking appearance. The windows have traditional divided lites, but in most cases they're limited to the top sash for uninterrupted views.

## A FLOOR PLAN WITH FLEXIBILITY

The bedrooms are on the darker northern side of the house to encourage sound sleep. The primary living areas are on the south side, making the spaces brighter and providing water views. There are living rooms, full bathrooms, and bedrooms on both floors, giving both the owners and guests privacy and allowing the owners to live on one level as they age.

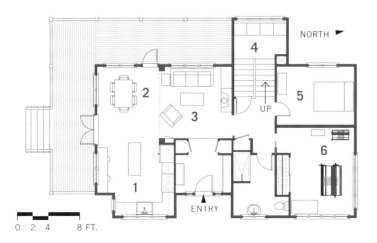

NORTH ▶

0  2  4        8 FT.

SPECS
**Bedrooms:** 2
**Bathrooms:** 2
**Size:** 2,100 sq. ft.
**Location:** Whidbey Island, Wash.
**Architect:** Matthew Swett,
         Taproot Architects,
         Langley, Wash., taproot.us
**Builder:** Sound Construction LLC,
         soundconstructionllc.com

### FIRST FLOOR

1 Kitchen            5 Bedroom
2 Dining             6 Weaving studio/
3 Parlor                future bedroom
4 Landing

## A HARDWORKING, COMPACT PLAN

It was a bit of a challenge to fit everything my clients wanted into the available area, but a few key decisions made it work. We split the living area across the floors. This resulted in a modest parlor on the lower floor and a more generous living room on the second floor, where there is better access to the views. This allowed us to closely follow the original house plan, with the bedrooms on the north side and the living areas on the south.

A small addition for the stairs provided just enough room for a walk-out laundry room on the first landing and a built-in window seat on the landing above.

We added a wraparound porch on the view side of the house. Aesthetically, this helped to shape the home into its farmhouse character. Functionally, the porch extends the living space outward,

providing shelter in inclement weather, and even transforming into a kennel for Loki and Sunna, the family dogs. Steel railings atop trolleys telescope out from behind fixed railings to close off the stairs. This provides an easy transition between human and canine needs. Last but not least, the structure of the porch discretely encloses 5,000 gal. of rainwater collection beneath it.

The scope of the renovation allowed us to address the issue of aging in place. The enlarged bathroom provides a wheelchair-friendly environment with a roll-in shower, and the weaving room can be utilized as a future master bedroom. These two features ensure that essential needs can be provided on the main floor. The few steps up from grade at the entry are a result of the existing foundation, but can easily be addressed with a modest ramp if and when needed.

## STAIR TOWER MAKES IT WORK

The second floor contains the master bedroom, a full bath, and a comfortable living
area with a propane fireplace. Like the first-
floor living room, the upstairs living area has
south-facing water views. The stair tower,
an 8-ft. by 10-ft. addition to the original
footprint, connects the first and second
floors and provides a refuge in the form of a
reading nook on its oversize landing.

**SECOND FLOOR**

1 Living area        4 Landing
2 Master suite      5 Storage
3 Closet            6 Mechanicals

## EFFICIENT SHELL, RECLAIMED DETAILS

Kathy and David's historic home in Seattle was chronically cold, so they wanted their new home to be more comfortable. We addressed that need with a quality building envelope and a multilayered heating system. The envelope contains R-28 double-stud walls filled with dense-pack cellulose, a high-R-value roof (R-59), and a better-than-code (R-38) floor system. Air leakage is a big part of envelope performance, so we taped the sheathing joints and used fluid-applied flashing around window and door openings.

To complement the envelope, we installed a heat-recovery ventilator to ensure the home has a steady supply of clean, fresh air. The ventilation system has high-performance filtration that helps keep pet fur and dander under control. The heating system consists of traditional floor-mounted radiators heated by an electric boiler coupled with radiant-tile heat mats and propane fireplaces to ensure that the home will stay warm, even in a power outage.

TOP: MORE THAN A STAIRWAY. The staircase to the second floor has a window seat at the landing—a perfect spot for reading a book or enjoying a cup of coffee. Underneath the landing is an 8-ft. by 10-ft. laundry room with grade-level access to the outdoors.

BOTTOM: MODERN BATH WITH TIMELESS APPEAL. The 10-ft. by 10-ft. upstairs bath has 1-in. hexagonal floor tile, period fixtures, and white subway tile that give the bath a historic look with modern conveniences. The toilet is tucked into an alcove adjacent to the shower.

## MAKING ROOM FOR INSULATION

The house has staggered double-stud walls filled with dense-pack cellulose insulation. The roof is also super-insulated with stacked pairs of rafters arranged like a truss with top and bottom chords. The deep space provides more room for cellulose insulation above the sloping ceiling and the space between the rafter pairs acts as a thermal break. The unusual rafter arrangement has a second benefit: The upper rafter creates the exposed rafter tail with the right proportions to complement the rest of the exterior.

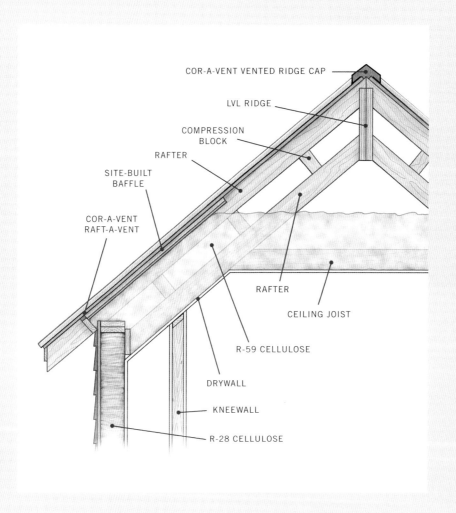

COR-A-VENT VENTED RIDGE CAP

LVL RIDGE

COMPRESSION BLOCK

RAFTER

SITE-BUILT BAFFLE

COR-A-VENT RAFT-A-VENT

RAFTER

CEILING JOIST

R-59 CELLULOSE

DRYWALL

KNEEWALL

R-28 CELLULOSE

## SALVAGED-STOCK INTERIOR

The original cabin's floors and walls were covered almost entirely with Douglas fir. We spent several months removing as much of the wood as we could with Burke bars and a host of pry bars. The boards were then resawn to create wainscoting, ceiling boards, and the coat rack and bench near the entrance. Some of the boards became walls in our workshop. The interior doors came from Ballard Reuse in Seattle. One side of the doors was varnished and the other heavily painted.

We used a low-temperature heat gun to remove the paint from the flat surfaces and 3M Safest Stripper on molded sections. After applying the stripper, we left it covered with plastic for 4 to 6 hours and then removed the softened paint with coarse steel wool and an assortment of scraping tools. After removing the paint, we sanded the surface to 120 grit with a Bosch random-orbit sander. Smaller areas were sanded with a small belt sander and a Fein oscillating multitool. The smallest areas were sanded by hand. After the doors were finished with two coats of water-based polyurethane, a local craftsman prepped them and hung them on jambs. Whenever possible, we used period or reproduction hinges and hardware.

—Kathy Stetz, the homeowner

Climate change and seismic activity in our area continue to encourage us to think about how best to support personal and community needs in the event of disrupted services. In addition to the enhanced thermal envelope, this home also has a backup generator, heating system, and water storage on hand. The thinking is simple: If our needs are met, we are more available to help others in need.

My clients wanted a home that expressed their attention to craft and appreciation of materials. Much of the native fir used in the home was salvaged and resawn by a mill in nearby Port Townsend. The kitchen cabinets were hand-built in David's shop. Finish-carpentry details blend seamlessly into the architecture. My clients weren't spectators in this regard—Kathy spent countless hours restoring historic doors for use in the interior, while David used his woodworking skills to build the custom entry coat rack.

Overall, the house has a warm glow. It can be seen in the rich character of the interior and exterior woodwork, but it runs deeper. It's a feeling evoked when you walk through the space—it feels like home.

# NEW ENGLAND FARM-HOUSE FOR TODAY

A modern, high-performance farmhouse that fits an established neighborhood, has a timeless appeal, and will adapt to the lifestyle changes of its future homeowners

BY SEAN GROOM

FOR THE FINAL FARMHOUSE IN THIS FIRST SECTION, we feature a house that was designed and built as a demonstration home for *Fine Homebuilding* magazine. Over the last 40 years, *Fine Homebuilding* has been a residential building, remodeling, and design resource providing information about everything from basic construction skills to advanced building methods and cutting-edge design. When designer Michael Maines, builder Mike Guertin, and *Fine Homebuilding's* Rob Yagid sat down to sketch out ideas for this home in East Greenwich, R.I., they laid out basic goals: The house had to be modestly sized, energy smart, healthy, flexible, and durable. These targets guided the design process and the construction methods and products that Maines used.

## TIMELESS FARMHOUSE STYLE

The style of the traditional farmhouse was Maines' design inspiration for the home. The low eaves, achieved by tucking the second-floor bathrooms and laundry room into dormers on the front of the house, reduce its perceived height, bringing the home to scale with its neighbors. At the rear of the house, the saltbox-style roofline grants the three second-floor bedrooms full-height ceilings, taking advantage of the southern exposure and bringing sun deep into the rooms. The simple white clapboard siding fits the look of the neighborhood, but the shed dormer and the front entry—cladded with Boral 8-in.-wide nickel-gap siding painted a rich espresso with Sherwin Williams' Black Fox—is the first clue that this home is a modern take on the traditional farmhouse vernacular.

Wherever this siding is used, corner boards and casing are eliminated; the siding is butted to the windows and doors and outside corners are mitered. These crisp, modern details continue with the Feeney Cable Rail system on the nearly 400-sq.-ft. deck, which divides the modern treatment of the walkout from the traditional lap siding above. The 2-over-2 windows that Maines chose are appropriate to a classic 19th-century farmhouse, and by using them throughout the house he weaves the traditional and modern treatments into a unified contemporary aesthetic.

## THE ASSEMBLY AT A GLANCE

ROOF: 22 in. of blown-in fiberglass insulation in the attic provides R-60. CertainTeed's MemBrain, run across the bottom of the ceiling joists and sealed to the top plates, creates a continuous air barrier.

WALLS: Zip panels with taped joints act as the primary air barrier. Taped R-21 CertainTeed Smart-Batts act as a secondary air barrier. Exterior Roxul Comfortboard 80 prevents thermal bridging and reduces the chance of condensation on the interior.

FOUNDATION: Amvic Silverboard subslab insulation and the Amvic 3.3 ICFs insulate the basement to R-15 and R-30, respectively. Concrete is an effective air barrier and ProtectoWrap's Triple Guard Energy Sill Sealer air-seals the transition between the foundation and framing.

## ACCENTS SET THE STYLE

### DECK RAIL

From a distance, the Feeney Cable Rail system disappears from view, and up close the horizontal cables reinforce the lines of the lap siding. The fascia-mount metal guardrail posts are clean and minimalist. Under-rail LED lights discreetly light the deck without interrupting the clean lines of the railing.

### STONE BASE

A mix of three colors of Cultured Stone veneer mixed with small infill rocks from the site cover the foundation. The suggestion of a rubble foundation emphasizes the traditional farmhouse style. The dark siding above the stone on the walk-out level indicates it's a different type of space than the upper levels.

### TRIM

4-in.-wide casing with thick sills at window openings and 6-in.-wide corner boards create shadow lines and reinforce the traditional look of the clapboards. Omitting trim on the wall sections with dark nickel-gap siding and butting the siding to the windows and mitering the corners creates cleaner lines and focuses attention on the bigger siding reveals.

# A TRADITIONAL LOOK WITH LOW-MAINTENANCE MATERIALS

Building the home in the aesthetic of a traditional farmhouse dictated bevel siding and time-honored paint colors, but that didn't mean modern materials and methods were off the table. Engineered siding provides a durable, low-maintenance exterior, and the paint will last longer thanks to a ventilated rain-screen assembly. Accent siding with mitered corners and a deck with cable railings are signs that the traditional aesthetic gives way to a modern design in the interior. The contemporary feel there announces that the house isn't stuck in the past, but the lack of ornamentation and the monochromatic color scheme simplify maintenance in a rental property.

In keeping with the farmhouse design, most of the house is clad with a 4-in.-reveal clapboard siding painted a classic farmhouse white. This cladding and trim, Boral TruExterior, is a poly-ash exterior board made from a combination of refined coal fly ash, glass fibers, and polymers.

These poly-ash boards have several advantages over wood and PVC products. They aren't affected by moisture or heat, they're rated for ground contact, they can be painted dark colors, and their end cuts don't need to be primed or sealed. The material's performance is similar to fiber-cement siding, yet TruExterior is lighter—closer to the weight of wood—with a flexibility approaching that of PVC boards.

To add visual interest, designer Michael Maines chose a tongue-and-groove siding, TruExterior nickel gap, for the shed dormer. Run horizontally, detailed with mitered corners, and painted a warm gray, this accent siding not only provides an aesthetic break with the traditional clapboard on the rest of the house, but it also creates a fictional history that suggests both dormers were added at a later date. The same siding continues around the front door to help draw the eye to the entry.

The 1x3 strapping that holds the Roxul exterior insulation in place creates the ventilation space behind the siding (a best practice). At the top and bottom of the wall, Cor-A-Vent SV5 vents allow the passage of air and water. Furring creates a pocket at the corner boards and windows, much like a J-channel, so the bevel siding tucks behind the trim.

A facade of Boral Cultured Stone applied to the exposed foundation and as a wainscot around the walkout basement completes the farmhouse look. Maines selected a mix of three colors to blend with the local stone, which is used to create retaining walls around the site and to provide a traditional-looking foundation. To make the stone in plane with the siding

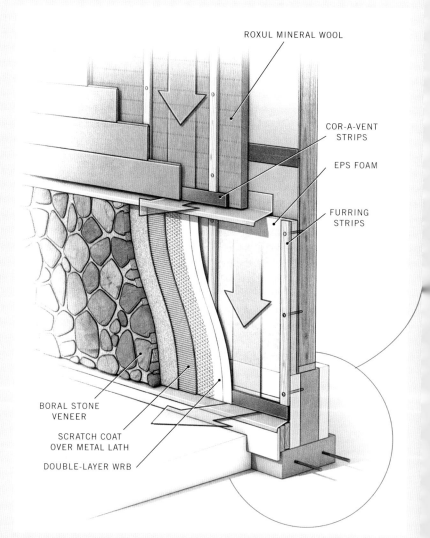

ROXUL MINERAL WOOL

COR-A-VENT STRIPS

EPS FOAM

FURRING STRIPS

BORAL STONE VENEER

SCRATCH COAT OVER METAL LATH

DOUBLE-LAYER WRB

above, builder Mike Guertin furred the stone out from the wall, creating an air gap between the exterior insulation and the water-resistive barrier (WRB) and metal lath that the scratch coat is applied to. (Areas where Cultured Stone is used require EPS rigid foam rather than the semicompressible Roxul mineral wool, which isn't an appropriate base for the heavy stone veneer.)

**Exterior Cladding Details**

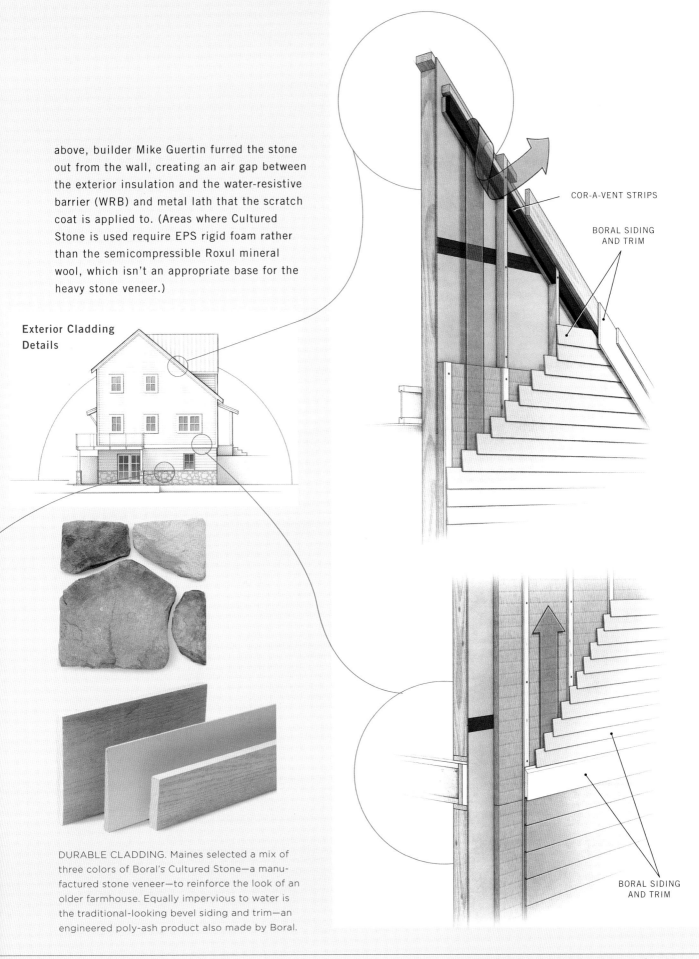

COR-A-VENT STRIPS

BORAL SIDING AND TRIM

BORAL SIDING AND TRIM

DURABLE CLADDING. Maines selected a mix of three colors of Boral's Cultured Stone—a manufactured stone veneer—to reinforce the look of an older farmhouse. Equally impervious to water is the traditional-looking bevel siding and trim—an engineered poly-ash product also made by Boral.

## A FLOOR PLAN FOR TODAY AND FOR TOMORROW

The most important aspect of the home is its ability to adapt over time as its occupants' lives change. The floor plan that Maines and interior designer Pamela Unwin-Barkley developed provides options to accommodate a growing family, multigenerational living, empty nesters, and those who wish to age in place.

For now, this means that with the partially finished basement and the bonus room over the garage, the house has a phenomenal amount of storage space. However, the framing, electrical, and plumbing rough-ins in the basement are ready for a self-contained apartment with a kitchen, full bath, bedroom, and large, open living area. Four tall windows on the south wall flood the basement's great room with natural light. If the basement is set up as an apartment, builder Mike Guertin will install a separate permeable-paver driveway from the street to the lower level that will provide single-level access and privacy to the in-law apartment. By finishing the underside of the deck and including an integral water-collection and gutter system, he has already created a covered entry and dry patio space.

The flex room, though, is the most intriguing space in the house. The configuration of pocket doors around the first-floor flex room and half bathroom may seem like overkill at first glance, but they serve two purposes. First, the doors into the flex room itself allow the room to be closed for privacy if, for example, someone is working from home. Plus, the second hallway pocket door allows the room to function as a small guest suite with a bedroom and half bath. Second, if the occupants ever decide on one-level living, the pocket door between the bathroom and the entry can be replaced with a wall and the half bath expanded into the pantry to create a full bathroom, converting the flex room into a first-floor master suite.

If additional space is needed on the second floor, the garage attic, which is insulated and drywalled, could provide about 284 sq. ft. of living space after adding 42-in. knee walls.

## FLEXIBILITY IN THE FLOOR PLAN

*Double duty* describes the home's first-floor open plan. The borders between the kitchen, dining, and living areas are fluid, with the intention that when any one of these spaces is in use, it can borrow additional room from the adjoining area. This allows the space to feel and function larger than its 425 sq. ft.

Storage can't be an afterthought in a smaller house. In this house's current configuration, there's plenty of storage space

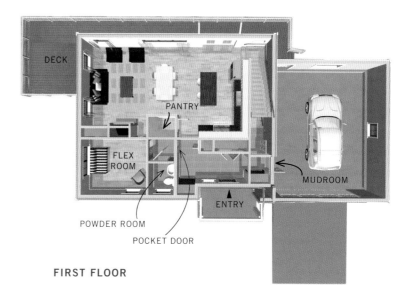

**FIRST FLOOR**

---

**SPECS**

**Bedrooms:** 3
**Bathrooms:** 2½
**Size:** 2,533 sq. ft.
**Completed:** 2017
**Location:** East Greenwich, R.I.
**Designer:** Michael Maines, michaelmaines.com
**Builder:** Mike Guertin

in the above-garage bonus area and in the basement. But if those areas are converted into living space, Maines has included other convenient storage for daily items throughout the plan, including the pantry in the kitchen, two closets off the front entry, a closet in the flex room, and a large walk-in closet in the master suite. Finally, the garage, which can be thought of as an oversize one-car garage, has plenty of additional room.

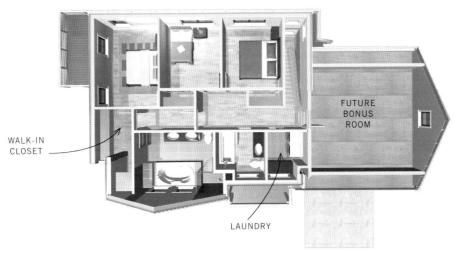

WALK-IN CLOSET

FUTURE BONUS ROOM

LAUNDRY

**SECOND FLOOR**

CLUTTER CUTTER. Garages tend to become dumping grounds for tools, toys, and seasonal items. Gladiator's storage system of cabinets, shelving, and wall storage provides organized storage and dedicated work space.

## FARM TABLE AT THE CENTER OF THE KITCHEN

When interior designer Pam Unwin-Barkley begins thinking of the space in a project, she considers both a client's needs and their things. "In effect," she relates, "I'm telling a story about who they are and how they live."

With this property, there is no specific client, so as she and Guertin discussed the interior design, they focused on the modern aspect of Maines' contemporary design. By using clean lines and a minimalist style, her goal was a timeless aesthetic that would weather changing design trends.

She chose a minimal trim package with drywall returns for the windows rather than casing. The door casings and baseboards have simple, flat profiles. The color palette of the Sherwin Williams paint used on the walls—light grays, soft blues, and pale greens with touches of cream and yellow—work together to create a light and airy interior. At the center of the first floor, a deep-gray tone (Sherwin Williams' Let it Rain) on the four pantry walls is a focal point, surrounded by related, softer tones on the perimeter, like the bluish Mountain Air in the kitchen.

GATHER HERE. Illuminated by Kichler fixtures, the large, multipurpose island with seating for three anchors the kitchen. Cosmopolitan White Caesarstone counters were chosen for their durability and natural warmth.

Just as the farmhouse theme drove the exterior design, it also guided Maines in the kitchen where he interpreted the classic farmhouse table as a modern island.

The kitchen island gives the room an L-shape that allows circulation during parties and room for two to work around each other. It also serves as a boundary, delineating the cooking space and separating it from the adjoining dining and living spaces. It is intentionally placed close to the front door and the garage entrance as a landing spot for groceries entering the house. And, to ensure there's plenty of storage in the kitchen, Maines incorporated a pantry near the stove end of the island.

The Shaker-style pine kitchen cabinets echo the three-panel, Shaker-style doors throughout the home, and the natural pine coordinates with the 5¼-in.-wide carbonized bamboo flooring.

MODERN MASTER. The crisp blue walls and clean lines and white surround of the soaking tub create a bright, airy, and welcoming master bath.

## A BIT OF LUXURY IN THE HARDEST-WORKING SPACES

The second floor of the home is a hardworking space. The bedrooms are only as large as they need to be, which allows a lot of amenities to be packed into the compact plan. In addition to two bedrooms, their associated full bath, and a laundry room, Maines also worked in a full master suite.

The bathrooms are an especially important design element in the house. Because they are used daily, the spaces shape the occupants' experience in the home.

In the full bathrooms, Unwin-Barkley chose 8x6 and 12x24 gray tiles for the floors with matching grout to play down the grid pattern. In the interest of comfortable winter mornings, Guertin installed ProtectoWrap's Peel and Heat Complete electric radiant heat mats before tiling the floors.

The master bath includes both a shower and a soaking tub for a bit of luxury. The shower has white, 2-in.-square mosaic floor tiles and stacked 3x9 horizontal tiles in a bond pattern that helps draw the eye horizontally around the room. The soaking tub is centered between the windows, both for the outdoor connection and to bring natural light into the room, which is reflected around the space by the vanity mirrors on the opposite wall. The tub deck, as well as the vanity top and

shower curb, are Caesarstone's Fresh Concrete, a light-colored surface with hardly any lines or veins. Without any grout lines or visible seams, the durable, solid-surface tops are easy to clean. Guertin took advantage of the area beneath the tub surround to add storage by building 12-in.-deep drawers into the front of the surround.

The other full bath has the same design sensibility, tweaked slightly for the space. Because the room is smaller, the 4x12 tile in the combination tub/shower runs vertically in order to draw the eye upward instead of horizontally, creating the perception of more space. These tiles have a raised curvilinear pattern that adds texture and interest and also emphasizes the vertical lines.

The choice of bathroom fixtures was driven by both performance and aesthetics. They had to be WaterSense qualified, which means third-party certified to be 20% more water efficient than the average fixture in their category while still performing as well or better than those less-efficient products. Aesthetically, the fixtures had to have clean, modern lines.

Both upstairs bathrooms have American Standard Town Square toilets with their Right Height design, which makes it easier to sit and stand from the toilet. The 1.28 gal. flush is water efficient, while the concealed trapway offers visually clean lines.

# Part 2

# FARMHOUSE KITCHENS

# A KITCHEN BUILT ON TRADITION

## Modernizing through the use of historical details

BY RAFE CHURCHILL

AS THE SON OF A SECOND-GENERATION MASTER builder, I'm continuing a family legacy of creating traditional homes inspired by the historic architecture of New England and taking it further through work that responds to both the landscape and the specific needs of each client. My firm creates what has become known as the "new old house"—a building offering modern amenities, but with the scale, proportions, and textures of a historic home.

That approach to design and construction served as the foundation of this kitchen's redesign and reconstruction. The clients—a professional chef and an interior designer—wanted a new kitchen for their 1920s farmhouse that would have modern qualities as well as traditional ones to create a bright, welcoming, and comfortable atmosphere.

### UNDERSTATED DESIGN

My favorite kitchens are those found in old abandoned houses or those found in vintage farmhouses that have been untouched by overzealous remodelers. These kitchens were mostly built of freestanding cabinetry and simple wall-hung cupboards, and they included fully exposed appliances. Freestanding appliances imbue a kitchen with an unassuming simplicity, so we employ this design strategy where appropriate. In this kitchen, the range is built into the cabinetry, but a 48-in. stainless refrigerator with glass doors stands alone in the corner opposite the range. To make the kitchen appear older, we hung a single wall cupboard to the right of the sink to store glassware and introduced a shallow, freestanding hutch near the dining area for additional storage. In order to make so few upper cabinets possible, we relied on the nearby pantry cabinets, which are much larger, to handle the bulk of the kitchen's storage needs.

### SYMPATHETIC SURFACES

If there is one element within the kitchen that markedly establishes its country style, it's the paneling that covers the walls and ceiling, which were original to the farmhouse. Painted Benjamin Moore's Moonlight White, the paneling extends into the adjacent living areas of the home, creating a bright and continuous backdrop throughout the main floor. To complement the white walls, ceilings, and trim, we selected rift and quarter-sawn white-oak flooring and installed it throughout the pantry and the kitchen and into the living room. The flooring is light enough to keep the bright and open theme intact; plus it's durable, making it a good option for this dog-friendly home. We finished the flooring with Rubio Monocoat, a unique hard-wax oil.

SUBLIME SIMPLICITY. The remodel of this farm-house kitchen in northwest Connecticut evokes lessons in traditional design to create a welcoming space that's bright and comfortable.

## A CHEF'S KITCHEN

The client wanted the kitchen to function efficiently without spilling its prep areas into the dining area. In response, the range, refrigerator, and island are placed toward the north end of the kitchen, near the pantry. Meal prep and cooking can occur without too much interference, even when guests gravitate toward the island.

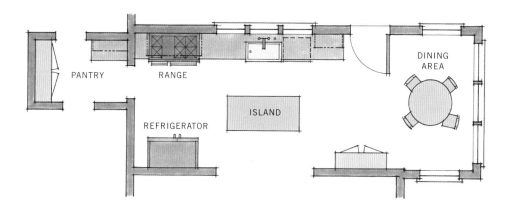

The countertops are the second-most prominent surface in the kitchen. The island top is made of 2-in.-thick premium wide-plank maple and has been oiled to give it a subtle contrast to the other countertops in the kitchen, which are—to the surprise of many—not soapstone. They're actually schist and have a beautifully rich gray color with slight veining throughout.

### CABINETRY AND COLOR

The details of the few cabinets and the burst of color they impart on the space reflect some of our other kitchen designs, which these clients were drawn to. We turn to Shaker sensibilities when designing cabinets for our kitchens, and this can produce a more modern aesthetic. The cabinets are locally made and feature simple beaded face frames, flat-panel doors, and solid drawer fronts. Wooden knobs and chrome bin pulls keep the cabinetry balanced and unified with the paneling

and flooring. The elements of this kitchen aren't competing for attention; rather, they are working together to create a simple space.

When it comes to color selections, I prefer colors that are more subdued and restrained. However, the clients presented tear sheets of various dream kitchens to use, and they kept gravitating toward one with light-blue cabinetry. In the end, they selected Farrow & Ball Green Blue for all of the cabinetry in the kitchen. It's a more modern color selection, which adds to the way this kitchen presents traditional elements that feel firmly rooted in the present.

BUILT FOR WORK. The kitchen's simplified arrangement doesn't come at the expense of functionality. A cook zone with a 48-in. Wolf range sits beneath a simply constructed custom hood. The schist backsplash extends to cover the entire wall surface behind the cooktop in order to make cleanup easy and to put its beautiful veining on display. Much of the kitchen's design is made possible by a pantry outfitted with floor-to-ceiling cabinetry. The pantry relieves the kitchen of an excess of upper cabinets and handles most of the bulk-food storage.

## SOURCES

CABINETS
Nichols Woodworking, Washington Depot, Conn.
nicholswoodworking.com

PENDANTS
CB2 Victory pendant (dining)
cb2.com
Olde Good Things vintage pendants (island)
ogtstore.com

COUNTERTOPS
Schist, Rock Solid Marble & Granite, Sheffield, Mass.
rocksolidmandg.com

PAINT
Farrow & Ball Green Blue (cabinets)
farrow-ball.com
Benjamin Moore Moonlight White (walls)
benjaminmoore.com
Kesl Brothers Painting, Canton, Conn.
keslbrotherspainting.com

SINK
Shaws Fireclay farm sink
rohlhome.com

RANGE
48-in. Wolf dual fuel
subzero-wolf.com

REFRIGERATOR
48-in. Sub-Zero

HARDWARE
Restoration Hardware (bin pulls)
restorationhardware.com
Shaker Workshops (wood knobs)
shakerworkshops.com

FLOORING
5-in. rift and quartersawn white oak,
Franklin Wood Products, Salisbury, Conn.
Rubio Monocoat clear finish
rubiomonocoatusa.com

# FROM CARDBOARD
# TO CABINETS

Fine-tuning
a kitchen
makeover
with card-
board mock-
ups dialed in
a delightful
design

BY CHARLES MILLER

SEATTLE'S WALLINGFORD NEIGHBORHOOD IS FILLED
with charming bungalows from the early 20th century, but when Craig
Zehnder and his wife, Amanda, were house-hunting, it was a 1901 farmhouse that caught their eye. It immediately reminded them both of the
rural farmhouses of their Michigan childhoods. Overall, the house was in
great shape for its age, but as an architect and craftsman, Craig saw it as
a blank canvas waiting for some creative updates.

Nothing was left of the original kitchen. Gutted and remodeled in the
early 1980s, the kitchen had been outfitted with inexpensive appliances
and cabinets, laminate countertops, and can lights. Along the south wall,
an awkward soffit topped the upper cabinets. The north wall was a blank.

At a basic level, the kitchen functioned, but it didn't have much appeal.
Plus, the Zehnders found that the lack of an effective range hood was a
nuisance, especially during intense cooking while entertaining family and
friends.

## MOVING THE BASEMENT DOOR UNCLOGS THE FLOOR PLAN

Typical of houses from this era, the door to the basement was in the
kitchen, wasting valuable floor space (see the before plan on p. 166).
Also, the refrigerator was jammed so close to the hall that it hid the
door casings.

After drawing several plans that tried to make the layout work with the
basement door, Craig finally had the inspiration to move the stair a few
feet to the east, with access off the hall. That freed space in the corner for
a full-height pantry, with plenty of room to hide the microwave and a large
pullout drawer for oversize items.

Moving the adjacent wall a few inches to the north gave the refrigerator a built-in look and allowed for doorway trim that matched the style of
the rest of the house.

To make sure the proportions of the new kitchen both looked and felt
right, Craig mocked it up in cardboard and used a black marker to sketch
out the cabinet faces and forms. This was an especially useful exercise for
the north wall, where the design called for a built-in hutch (photo facing
page). Because of the windows on the west wall, the hutch needed to be
shallower in depth than typical kitchen cabinets.

The new kitchen looks right at home in its 100-year-old surroundings.
The Zehnders are particularly proud when they have visitors who say that
it looks like it could be the original kitchen.

PROBLEM: Douglas-fir flooring too soft for the kitchen.

SOLUTION: A two-tone cork floor extends the warmth of the fir floors into the kitchen, but the cork is more durable and easy to clean. Even the occasional tennis-ball soccer match with the homeowners' golden retriever hasn't scratched the cork.

KITCHEN BEFORE

**ABOVE**: PROBLEM: Incorrectly proportioned cabinets.

**RIGHT**: SOLUTION: Cardboard
mock-ups of all the cabinets and
counters allowed in-place evalu-
ations and easy revisions where
necessary.

**"AHA!"MOMENT**

Moving a staircase is a pretty big deal in a small remodel, but
sometimes the benefits so clearly outweigh the drawbacks that it's
undeniably the right decision. Relocating the stair to the nearby
hallway made the entire corner to the left of the range available
for drawers, a pantry, and more counter space.

**BEFORE**

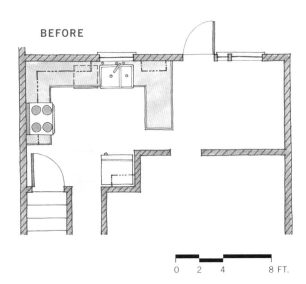

0  2  4      8 FT.

**AFTER**

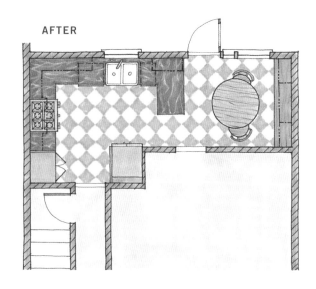

ABOVE: PROBLEM: Lackluster details unsuited to the farmhouse style and a useless recirculating range hood.

RIGHT: SOLUTION: A restrained palette of Douglas-fir ceiling boards, cork floors, white subway tiles, and enameled cabinetry carries the original detailing found throughout the house into the kitchen. In the hutch (p. 165), wavy antique glass from old single-pane windows nails the early 20th-century look. The new 1200-cfm hood that vents to the exterior successfully clears cooktop air.

## NOTABLE ELEMENTS

**COUNTERS:** honed Vermont Verde Antique marble

**FLUSH-MOUNT LIGHT FIXTURES:** Rejuvenation

**TWO-TONE CORK FLOOR:** Expanko

**APRON SINK:** Shaw

**CABINET PULLS:** Alno satin nickel

**RANGE:** BlueStar

COOL DETAIL. Glass shelves in the built-in hutch allow light from fixtures at the top of the cabinet to pass through to the counter, illuminating goblets and glassware.

# TRADITIONAL AT FIRST GLANCE

With hints of the Shaker style, this kitchen's more modern leanings are subtle, but important

BY BRIAN PONTOLILO

NESTLED IN THE HEART OF WESTCHESTER COUNTY, Bedford, N.Y., is within reasonable commuting distance to Manhattan with its own stop on Metro-North Railroad's Harlem Line. To those not familiar with the landscape of New York's Hudson Valley, that may conjure images of cookie-cutter neighborhoods. The area is home to many of New York City's daily refugees, but it is also home to farmland, dirt roads, and some of the most charming antique houses in the country.

This kitchen is in one such home. A homesteader's dwelling originally built in 1830, the house started as an understated, one-and-a-half-story farmhouse and was remodeled and added onto regularly over its nearly 200-year history, most recently when it was purchased by a family with three young children. They were attracted to the idyllic stream that runs through the property, the backyard pool where their children could make summertime memories, and the house's storied character. Charming as it was, it would take some work to make the house livable for the new family, who like to entertain. The kitchen would have to do some heavy lifting.

To help get the design right, the owners hired Rafe Churchill. Rafe is a co-founder of Hendricks Churchill, an architecture and interior design firm in Sharon, Conn., and is fluent in early American architecture and the new/old-home aesthetic.

"This was clearly an evolved house," Rafe explains. "The last family owned the house for 40 years, and it had been shaped to their changing family needs. The goal was to start over and to make it work for this family, and to accommodate guests."

### KITCHEN ADDITION

Starting over in a protected home means starting over with sensitivity. To make the kitchen work spatially, Rafe designed a 16-ft. 6-in. by 6-ft. 8-in. bump-out addition. This was the only part of the project that included a change in footprint, but it still required approval because the house sits squarely in a historic district. The long run of custom Marvin windows is one detail that helped to tie the new addition to the rest of the house.

THE CLEAN LOOK OF SOAPSTONE. The kitchen is tied together with a deep-green soapstone used for the counters, backsplash, and sink. The stone is appropriate for the house's historic vintage and connects the lighter-colored interior finishes to the window color and landscape beyond. An oversize custom sink is a must-have once you've lived with one, the architect says.

Rafe's goal for the windows on projects like this is to maintain the same pane proportions as the original windows. He says that the height-to-width ratio of the lites is the most significant detail to maintain. In this case, he also kept the 8-over-8 lite patterns of the double-hung windows. The window sash color is Farrow & Ball's Down Pipe, a deep charcoal with some green in it, similar to the Essex Green and Black Forest Green commonly found on the doors and shutters of historic homes throughout the Northeast.

The large bank of windows helped to meet another of the homeowner's goals—a light-filled interior. "They wanted as much natural light as possible in the kitchen," Rafe says. "What's nice is the sunlight is indirect"—the windows face northeast.

The window color pairs well with the soapstone used for the counters, backsplash, and custommade sink. Not only does the sink have a seamless look and the stylish farmhouse aesthetic many are after, it is oversize at 2 ft. 9½ in. across the front, 1 ft. 4 in. front to back, and 10 in. deep. Rafe has a similar sink in his home and is enthusiastic about its performance.

"One you have one of these, you wonder how you ever lived with a regular 30-in. sink," he says. "Soapstone is soft, and the sink will stain and chip and develop a patina and that all adds to the authenticity."

The black-walnut island counter has an oil finish. It is food-safe, but not as durable as some other options, and therefore will also age naturally. Similarly, the unlacquered-brass cabinet hardware from Rejuvenation and faucet from Waterworks will take on a living finish, appropriate for a house of this age. Rafe mentions that if you don't want them to wear, it's important to make sure to order hardware and fixtures with a finish.

## SHAKER MODERN

While the kitchen island is set apart from the cabinetry and designed to appear as a freestanding piece of furniture, the cabinetry recalls the simplicity of the Shaker style.

"There's no doubt that the word Shaker was thrown around a little," Rafe says of his interactions with the homeowners. "But at the same time, they wanted the kitchen to feel more contemporary."

Rafe says that the Shaker style was ahead of its time, always pared down and understated. He explains how, if you subtly change the dimensions of the cabinet's face frames and the doors' stiles and rails, you can easily shift toward a more contemporary look. And that is what he did in this case.

"Shaker stiles would likely be more like 2¼ in., or even 2½ in. wide. Rails might be as wide as 1½ in.," he explains. "Here, the stile dimensions are 1¾ in. wide. The rails are 1¼ in. wide."

The custom cabinetry was built by a local company, R.C. Torre Construction, and the cabinets and millwork are finished with Farrow & Ball's Dove Tale. The island is painted with the company's Manor House Gray.

There are a few more details that lend to the kitchen's modern look, including the Sub-Zero fridge, Wolf range, and pair of Muuto pendants that hang over the island. The new flooring is white oak finished with Dinesen oil. The bar stools are a vintage find and a place where the homeowners' kids regularly hang out in the kitchen. Kathryn Fagin of KJ Designs was the interior designer on the project and helped with many of these selections.

One interesting decision was to lower the kitchen floor. After completing the addition, Rafe was standing in the space during a meeting with the owners. Rafe is a tall man and his presence made them aware of how low the kitchen ceiling was. By the end of the meeting, they had determined to take up and lower the floor. This meant reducing the number of steps leading from the entry into the kitchen and adding steps connecting the kitchen to the dining room and a hallway.

"When a house evolves like this one has, you often get all of these steps happening," Rafe explains. "In this case we were able to remove one step, which made a big difference. So, by dropping the floor, we improved the flow. Because having a step at one end of the kitchen was a little unusual, and now there are steps in other locations, it makes more sense. It created the expectation of steps into and out of the kitchen. It's also a nice way to define the space. The kitchen was large enough to handle a step up."

This kitchen is a wonderful example of subtle design, true to the Shaker ideal of simplicity, but updated for modern time. Rafe says the home-owners' interest in refining the details and design-ing a kitchen that worked for the family was refreshing and more fun than working in a vacuum. And clearly, expectations were set. It can't be any other way in a kitchen that is meant to wear well.

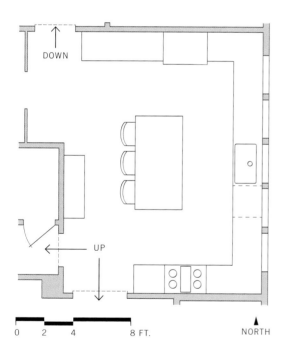

## STEP BY STEP BY DESIGN

The kitchen's floor plan is straightforward—the refrigerator, sink, and range create a work triangle that radiates around the island. The homeowners asked for a few particulars, like a pantry and coffee station, but their most significant request was for taller ceilings. The only viable path was to lower the floor. Now the kitchen is defined by a step separating it from all adjacent spaces.

# Part 3

# A GALLERY OF FARMHOUSES

# TEXAS HOMESTEAD REVIVED

## Shoring up a flimsy foundation and frame salvaged this rustic charmer

BY KILEY JACQUES

DESIGNER/BUILDER
Laughlin Homes
+ Restoration,
hillcountrybuilder.com

LOCATION
Johnson City, Texas

PHOTOS
Sarah Moore-Natsumi,
courtesy of Laughlin Homes
+ Restoration

BUILT IN 1904, THIS IS ONE OF THE ORIGINAL farmhouses found along Old Austin Highway. Its uninsulated plank construction—top plate, bottom plate, and 1x12s with battens—was less familiar to designer/builder Richard Laughlin than the framing he typically sees. "The house is just 30 miles away from most of our jobs, but it was built in a totally different era," he says. "People were poor and they had to make do with what they had."

To strengthen the walls, Laughlin added infill framing, creating an insulation cavity as well as a wiring cavity. The floor system was in bad shape, too. It sat on a stacked-rock foundation—the joists were either in the rubble or sitting on soil and, like the sills and subfloor, were in various stages of rot. To stabilize the structure and seal for moisture control, Laughlin pulled up the entire floor, leveled the building, and excavated to pour a concrete slab with foundation footings to support point loads inside the building. He replaced the joists with 2x4 sleepers over the new slab and reinstalled the original hardwood floorboards to be in keeping with the period.

"When we are working on these old houses, we try to go back in with period-appropriate materials to match the patina of the original products."
—Richard Laughlin, designer/builder

# A MODERN FARMHOUSE CONFORMS TO A TIGHT LOT

## This four-bedroom home gets the stature it deserves while meeting tough zoning regulations

BY KILEY JACQUES

DESIGNER
Clark Richardson Architects
clarkrichardson.com

BUILDER
Hudson Design
Development
hudsondesigndevelopment.
com

LOCATION
Austin, Texas

PHOTOS
Paul Finkel, courtesy of
Clark Richardson Architects

PRESENTED WITH A TIGHT URBAN LOT THAT NEEDED
to accommodate a four-bedroom/four-bathroom home, Clark Richardson
Architects conceived a strongly vertical two-gabled modern farmhouse.
The city of Austin's height and building-area constraints were a constant
battle. The challenge was to maintain a cost-effective structural design,
address the desire for high ceilings throughout, drain the deck area effec-
tively, and do all of this in an aesthetically pleasing manner.

The solution included a "habitable attic"—an open, vaulted space daylit by dormers—on the third floor that conforms to local code exemptions. The finished attic opens directly onto a floating wood deck atop a recessed roof surface, which allows water to drain directly into the gutter running the length of the primary gable. For a pleasing overall look, gables clad with white fiber-cement siding are outlined in black metal paneling, which wraps into the carport at the front entry, transitioning from roof to wall and down to grade.

# RESTORING THE ABIAH TAYLOR HOUSE

## It took careful archaeological detective work to reproduce original details for this historic home in Pennsylvania's Brandywine Valley

BY KILEY JACQUES

DESIGNER
John Milner Architects,
johnmilnerarchitects.com

LOCATION
Chester County, Pa.

PHOTOS
Don Pearse, courtesy of
John Milner Architects

BUILT IN 1724 ON THE EAST BANK OF THE BRANDY-wine River, the Abiah Taylor House was modified in several stages between 1780 and 1910. For John Milner Architects to restore it to its original state, "archaeological investigations" were required. For example, because the masonry openings remained intact when the original casement windows were removed during the 19th century, the architect found impressions of the original frames and pieces of original glass and lead muntins, which together were used to inform the design of the reconstructed windows. Similarly, interior and exterior paint colors were recreated based on microscopic paint analysis, and fragments of the original hand-sawn white-oak flooring on the first and second floors provided inspiration for the size and configuration of the new replacement flooring.

Other missing original features included exterior cornices, a pent roof (a small, single-slope roof above the first-floor windows), and paneled doors, plus sections of interior woodwork and flooring. These, too, were reconstructed based on architectural evidence, early photographs, and local precedent.

Housing the kitchen and master suite, the new addition has dark-stained clapboard siding rather than brick, so it doesn't compete with the original house. The new building touches the historic house in as narrow a profile as possible so as not to conceal the original form and materials.

# PROTECTION FROM SOLAR GAIN

This Pennsylvania farmhouse-style home uses sliding-shade screens to allow in daylight without too much heat

BY KILEY JACQUES

DESIGNER
Cutler Anderson Architects,
cutler-anderson.com

BUILDER
Frank Truncali of
Breig Bros.

LOCATION
Northeastern Pa.

PHOTOS
DavidSundberg@ESTO,
except Edith Green–Wendell
Wyatt Federal Building by
Nik Lehoux, courtesy of
Cutler Anderson Architects

SITUATED IN AN OPEN FIELD, THIS SIMPLE GABLE structure is oriented due south toward a pastoral view. The form is reminiscent of the homes common in northeastern Pennsylvania, which is dotted with hardscrabble farms. Staying true to the vernacular farmhouse style meant leaving off deep overhangs that would otherwise protect from summertime heat gain; eaves in this region are rarely more than 8 in. Instead, Cutler Anderson Architects designed sliding-shade screens on barn-door hardware that act like a straw hat, while six custom-built swinging doors on the south side and two on the north side support passive cross ventilation.

The inspiration for the approach came from a previous project by the same firm, namely the 18-story Edith Green–Wendell Wyatt Federal Building in Portland, Oregon (bottom left photo, facing page). That transformation of a 1970s concrete commercial building included re-cladding the entire structure in a curtainwall that hangs 22 in. beyond the perimeter of the existing structure. Fixed sunshades on the south side and vertical aluminum rods on the west elevation create an elaborate shading system. In this residential application, a pleasant degree of daylight is maintained, yet the screens yield a 15° temperature differential.

# BACK TO PLUMB AND IN PLANE

Creative framing and trim details straighten out the kinks during the remodel of a crooked old timber-frame farmhouse in Vermont

BY KILEY JACQUES

DESIGNER
Sustainable Design, LLC,
sdvermont.com

BUILDER
ReDesign Construction,
redesignconstruction.com

LOCATION
Chester, Vt.

PHOTOS
Christine Glade
Photography

THE TEAMS BEHIND THE RESTORATION OF THIS GREEK Revival farmhouse, Sustainable Design and ReDesign Construction, had two key issues to remedy. First, they had to level the top plate of the old timber frame to accept new raised-heel trusses. After identifying the extent to which the frame had shifted out of plumb and out of level, they reduced the distance between the plates by pulling together the existing beams with winches and come-alongs, jacking up extreme low spots, and trimming down high spots. Then they built new sloped cripple walls to level up the rest of the plates to match the highest point on the building.

Second, they needed to trim old, out-of-plumb walls with new door-ways and doors. Because the discrepancies were more than an inch, they ran the jambs level from the extents of the out-of-plumb wall, and then built out the back of the trim—like a reverse extension jamb—to bring it into plane with the wall and fill the void. Additionally, the team removed the plaster covering the original fireplaces and installed new hearths and timber-beam mantels, leaving the brick unpointed for an aged look. The stone fireplace is new.

# A MULTIPURPOSE PLAN

A number of cost-saving measures results in a well-organized farmhouse and separate guest dwelling built on a tight budget

BY KILEY JACQUES

DESIGNER
Burr and McCallum
Architects,
burrandmccallum.com

BUILDER
Eric Zahn Builders,
ericzahnbuilders.com

LOCATION
Great Barrington, Mass.

PHOTOS
Steve Bronstein

THE OWNERS OF THIS CONTEMPORARY FARMHOUSE approached Burr and McCallum Architects with ideas for an efficient, modestly sized, well-insulated house. The design program needed to accommodate a private residence, an art studio (one of the homeowners is a commercial photographer, the other is a graphic designer), and a potential rental unit—and it all had to be accomplished on a tight budget. In response, the team designed two structures: a compact, highly organized main house (top photo, facing page); and a separate dwelling that incorporates living space, which can be used either as guest house or a rental (bottom photo, facing page). The two buildings are located as close to each other as code allows, and a porch shelters most of the walkway between them. This arrangement creates a pleasant entry courtyard.

Cost-saving measures included using concrete-slab floors in some areas, spec'ing standard plumbing fittings and fixtures, buying manufactured dressers and building them into the bedrooms, sourcing an interior window from a salvage yard, and installing a small woodburning stove in lieu of a full fireplace.

# RETROFIT OF A TIMBER-FRAME FARMHOUSE

## A design/build team performs a small miracle on a dilapidated 1850s home

BY KILEY JACQUES

DESIGNER/BUILDER
Garland Mill,
garlandmill.com

LOCATION
Lancaster, N.H.

PHOTOS
Fletcher Manley,
courtesy of Garland Mill

THE OWNERS OF THIS NEW HAMPSHIRE GEM contacted Garland Mill to perform a small miracle on the dilapidated 1850s Shaker-style farmhouse. The design-build team was able to save the hand-hewn hemlock framing in a number of locations. They clad the exterior with clapboards and corner boards, installed two-over-one single-hung simulated-divided-lite windows, and built a frieze to encapsulate the original rafter plate, which sits proud of the wall and is characteristic of this style of timber-frame construction.

The interiors were given a modern treatment that is bare of baseboards and has minimal finishes. The soffited ceilings in the kitchen envelop the timber structure, which was unsightly. The dining room features reclaimed birch flooring and plaster windowsills and returns.

The original roof-framing system in the upstairs bedrooms juxtaposes contemporary built-in plaster bookshelves with floating birch planks, and transom windows above the doors steal light from the east and west gable windows. The blue plank floor was taken up and refinished to replicate the original, and additional built-in bookshelves and plaster returns line the ample hallway. Hand-hewn full-length joists and a heat-pump wall cassette peek out from the living room at the end of the hall. The entire house is a smooth blend of 1800s construction, contemporary detailing, and performance-enhancing measures.

# ABSTRACT EFFECT

## A complete remodel reinvented the home without altering its original form

BY KILEY JACQUES

DESIGNER
Waechter Architecture,
waechterarchitecture.com

BUILDER
Modern Urban
Development

LOCATION
Portland, Ore.

PHOTOS
David Papazian

TO BREATHE NEW LIFE INTO THIS 1910 FARMHOUSE-style home located in an urban neighborhood, Waechter Architecture maintained the original single-gable form but abstracted it for a modern feel. The traditional interior layout was reimagined as one main room per floor. Support spaces were used to create a "thickened edge" into which new windows were cut, with glass set to the inside. The result is rooms that feel protected and private. On the exterior, the 2-ft.-deep windowsills give the illusion of having been carved out. The monochromatic-red color scheme enriches economical cladding materials that include lap siding.

"The Red House serves as an example of progressive architecture that meets contemporary demands while preserving historic forms."

—Ben Waechter, principal

# CELEBRATING EFFICIENT POST-AND-BEAM CONSTRUCTION

**An old barn is transformed into a high performance home that highlights the structure's original framing**

BY KILEY JACQUES

DESIGNER
Bluetime Collaborative,
bluetimecollaborative.com

INTERIOR DESIGNER
Joanne Palmisano Design,
joannepalmisano.com

BUILDER
Webster Construction
and Helm Construction
Solutions, buildhelm.com

LOCATION
Southern Vermont

PHOTOS
Lindsay Selin Photography,
lindsayselinphotography.
com

WHAT BEGAN AS A DARK, OLD BARN-TURNED-hunting cabin is now a light-filled high-performance home. The idea was to celebrate the framing structure, pay homage to the building's history, and better its overall performance.

In the kitchen, subway tile lends a classic look, but bringing it up to the ceiling—beneath and above the beams—gives it a modern feel, and calls attention to the framing. The original stairs were relocated, and the second-floor loft was reconfigured to allow for two small bedrooms and a bathroom. The middle room is centered on the window, which was enlarged, and on the peak of the gable roof. A beam crosses in front of the newly enlarged window in yet another effort to highlight the old barn structure.

Some of the original siding was reclaimed to create oversize barn-door sliders, which not only provide privacy for the once-open bedroom but are an eye-catching design feature when viewed from the living room below. Other repurposed materials include the mirror above the bed, which had been the living-room window.

In addition to the aesthetic successes, the home's energy performance was drastically improved. The initial blower-door test result was a whopping 23 ACH50. Adding a smart air barrier and vapor-control layer, beefing up the insulation with dense-pack cellulose, installing double-pane Marvin All Ultrex windows and doors, and replacing existing siding with locally sourced raw hemlock vertical siding, among other upgrades, brought the house up to 2.3 ACH50. It's an energy-lean visual charmer, to say the least.

# WINDOWS ON THE FARMHOUSE

## A cost-effective, alternative installation for a house with exterior insulation

BY KILEY JACQUES

DESIGNER
Harry Hunt Architects,
harryhuntarchitects.com

BUILDER
Patterson Smith
Construction,
pattersonsmith.com

LOCATION
Stowe, Vt.

PHOTOS
Jim Westphalen
Photography, courtesy of
Harry Hunt Architects

"I set out to invent some new residential construction details that would optimize the constructability, cost effectiveness, and aesthetics of Joe's wall."
—Harry Hunt,
Harry Hunt Architects

CHARGED WITH DESIGNING A COST-EFFICIENT near–Passive House in climate zone 4, Harry Hunt Architects looked to building scientist Joseph Lstiburek's "Perfect Wall," which includes exterior insulation and puts the air and water barriers inboard of it, on the outside face of the sheathing (see p. 124). Rather than doing "outie" windows and doors with deep window bucks or structural extensions—a common choice among Vermont builders who use Lstiburek's assembly—Hunt opted for innie openings, which put the window flanges against the sheathing. This method, he says, is more cost-effective and easier to build. It also has aesthetic implications, particularly in New England where tradition calls for windows at the face of the wall.

There's a perception that deeply set windows and doors are a modern-style design element, but Hunt proves they can work in a farmhouse vernacular, too. He feels that this home's "traditional essence" has much to do with the window proportions and composition, and that where the openings sit in the wall does not diminish that. Additionally, he believes the more depth a facade has, the more interesting it is; and innie windows and doors add depth by creating shadowlines and breaking up flat planes.

# A UNIQUE FARMHOUSE COMPLEX

A pair of reno-
vated cabins
and a gathering
place for enter-
tainment are at
the heart of
this gem of a
farmstead

BY MAUREEN FRIEDMAN

DESIGNER
Zach Gasper, GreenSpur,
greenspur.net

CONSTRUCTION
GreenSpur

LOCATION
Virginia

PHOTOS
Mitch Allen,
mitchallenphotography.com,
courtesy of GreenSpur

## TWO CABINS BECOME ONE

Now one unique 1,800-sq.-ft. home, this farmhouse was originally two cabins built side-by-side 10 ft. from each other. The right side was a log cabin built in the late 1700s and was the first building on the property. Sometime in the early 1800s, an identically sized stone cabin was built next to the log cabin. Years ago, previous owners added a central doorway and an exterior wall between the cabins to make the two structures one.

Wanting to update the interior and exterior of the home, the current owners contacted GreenSpur, a local design firm. The team from Green-Spur began by removing the patchwork infill connecting the two cabins. To emphasize the original form and material of each of the cabins, they replaced the infill with a modern glass atrium that serves as the new entry. To better insulate the leaky log cabin, all of the chinking was removed to expose the bare wood. Rigid insulation was added to the cavities and sealed in place with spray foam, and new chinking was added inside and out. Radiant flooring now helps to heat the house in winter.

The 7-ft. first-floor ceiling heights in both buildings were raised to a more comfortable 8 ft., except on the far end of the log-cabin side, where the floor above the living room was removed to create a 26-ft.-high ceiling. All of the cabinetry, built-ins, and most of the furniture in the house were made with wood salvaged from a three-board fence found on the property. This mix of minimalism and historical textures balances both the old and the new.

## EVERYTHING UNDER THE SUN FOR FUN

Delighted with the changes to the house, the homeowners then hired GreenSpur to refashion an antique barn on their property into a multifac-eted outdoor entertainment complex (see pp. 198–199). Inspiration for the complex came from the antique bank barn on the property and the history of the farm itself. After a timber expert assessed the early 1800s structure as being in excellent condition for its age, the 30x40 barn was converted to a dining and dance hall. Renovations included bringing electricity to the barn and creating new openings in the front and at one side of the barn. The lumber from these cut-out sections, along with wood from a three-board fence found on the property, were used to construct the sliding barn doors.

Included in the plan for the complex were a pool and a pool house. A grain silo once sat adjacent to the barn, and though it had been removed long ago, a new silo was built in its place. Erected in one day, the 24-ft.-dia. silo is insulated with closed-cell spray foam and is heated and cooled with a ductless minisplit. A whiskey bar on the first floor serves as the socializ-ing center and hub for the outdoor space and as a connection to the barn.

PICTURE PERFECT. The stone around the hot tub and the silo foundation was found on the property. A bridge off the whiskey room connects the silo to the barn. The property formerly was owned by botanist Joseph Russell Smith, who in the 1920s wrote a book emphasizing the importance of mature trees in farming and soil preservation. As an ode to Smith's philosophy, mature trees were planted around the site and uplit at night.

FACING PAGE BOTTOM: SWEET RETREAT.
A slab was poured in the area below the barn so that the space could be used as a shaded hideaway to escape the summer sun.

THE MANY LEVELS OF SILO LIVING. For easy access to the pool and hot tub, the changing area and spa are located on the ground floor. The whiskey room and kitchen are on the first floor. A bedroom and bath are found on the second floor, and a studio is on the third floor.

GREAT VIEWS, DAY OR NIGHT. With the barn doors open, great views of the main house and pond, the pool, and the hot tub can be captured from the dining and dance hall.

# CONTRIBUTORS

**RAFE CHURCHILL** is a designer in Sharon, Conn.

**JEFFREY DOLAN** is a co-founder of Period Architecture in West Chester, Pa.

**JEREMIAH ECK,** FAIA, is a partner at EcklMacNeely Architects in Boston and the author of *The Distinctive Home* (The Taunton Press, 2003) and *The Face of Home* (The Taunton Press, 2006).

**MAUREEN FREEDMAN** is the former administrative assistant of *Fine Homebuilding*.

**R. ANDREW GARTHWAITE,** AIA, is principal at Haynes & Garthwaite Architects in Norwich, Vt.

**SEAN GROOM** is a contributing editor at *Fine Homebuilding*.

**PAUL HAGMAN,** AIA, is the founder of RBF CoLab Architecture and Design in Youngstown, Ohio.

**KILEY JACQUES** is senior editor of Green Building Advisor.

**DIANE KOLAK** is a freelance graphic designer in Michigan.

**MICHAEL MAINES** is a contributing editor at *Fine Homebuilding*.

**IAN MCDONALD,** AIA, is an architect on Shelter Island, N.Y. (www.ianmcdonaldarchitect.com).

**CHARLES MILLER** is *Fine Homebuilding* editor at large.

**MATT O'MALIA,** AIA, is the principal of OPAL, an architecture firm in Belfast, Maine.

**JUSTIN PAULY,** AIA, is an architect in Monterey, Calif.

**BRIAN PONTOLILO** is editorial director of *Fine Homebuilding*.

**MATT RISINGER** and **ERIC RAUSER,** AIA, design, build, and geek out on building science at Risinger & Co. in Austin, Texas.

**CLAY SMOOK,** AIA, is the founder of SMOOK Architecture & Urban Design.

**MATTHEW SWETT** is owner of Taproot Architects in Langley, Wash.

**ROB WHITTEN,** AIA, founded Whitten Architects in 1986.

**ROB WOTZAK** is *Fine Homebuilding's* digital brand manager.

# CREDITS

**pp. 2–9: The Beloved Farmhouse** by Michael Maines, FHB issue 269.

**p. 3:** photo by Rob Lagerstrom, courtesy of *The Progressive Farmer*

**p. 4:** photos by Susan Teare
DESIGN: Classic Home, classichomevt.com
BUILD: Classic Home, classichomevt.com
LOCATION: Charlotte, Vt.

**p. 5:** photos by Jeff Lendrum
DESIGN: Craig Sachs, AIA
BUILD: Mark Stoltz, Stoltz Construction, Wausau, Wis.
LOCATION: Waupaca, Wis.

**p. 6:** photos by Rob Lagerstrom, courtesy of *The Progressive Farmer*
DESIGN: Rehkamp Larson Architects, rehkamplarson.com
BUILD: Dovetail Renovation, Inc., dovetailrenovation.com
LOCATION: Lake City, Minn.

**p. 7:** photos by Whit Preston
DESIGN: Eric and Rebekah Rauser, Rauser Design, rauserdesign.com
BUILD: Risinger & Co., Risinger Homes, risingerhomes.com
LOCATION: Austin, Texas

**p. 8:** photos by Jim Westphalen
DESIGN: TruexCullins Architecture + Interior Design, truexcullins.com
BUILD: O'Neill Builders, gogreenoneill.com
LOCATION: Jericho, Vt.

**p. 9:** photos by Whit Preston
DESIGN: Tim Cuppett Architects, cuppettarchitects.com
BUILD: Wilmington Gordon, wilmington-gordon.com
LOCATION: Austin, Texas

**pp. 12–19: Four-Part Farmhouse** by Clay Smook, FHB issue 293. Photos by Benjamin Cheung, courtesy of SMOOK Architecture & Urban Design. Floor plan drawings by Patrick Welsh.

**pp. 20–27: How Great Houses Take Shape** by Jeremiah Eck, FHB issue 195. Photos by Charles Miller except for photos pp. 21 and 24 by Eric Roth. Floor plan drawings by Martha Garstang Hill.

**pp. 28–35: A Colonial Resurrection** by Jeffrey Dolan, FHB issue 251. Photos by Charles Bickford, except inset photo p. 29 courtesy of Jeffrey Dolan. Sidebar drawings pp. 30–31 by Dan Thornton; floor plan drawings p. 31 by Martha Garstang Hill.

**pp. 36–43: Modern Masonry Farmhouse** by Charles Miller, FHB issue 235. Photos by Richard Leo Johnson, except for photos p. 38 by Charles Miller; pp. 39, 40 (model), and 41 by Tina Govan; and p. 42 courtesy of Kelly Finch. Floor plan drawings by Martha Garstang Hill.

**pp. 44–49: Federal Farmhouse** by R. Andrew Garthwaite, FHB issue 267. Photos by GBH Photography (gbhphotography.com). Drawings p. 47 by Christopher Mills; floor plan drawings p. 49 by Martha Garstang Hill.

**pp. 50–57: Rural Landscape, Modern Sensibility** by Diane Kolak, FHB issue 203. Photos by Brian Confer, except for inset photo p. 51 by Diane Kolak. Floor plan drawings by Martha Garstang Hill.

**pp. 58–65: Resurrecting a Greek Revival** by Paul Hagman, FHB issue 275. Photos by David Pokrivnak (pokrivnak.com) courtesy of RBF CoLab, except for inset photo p. 59 courtesy of the homeowners. Floor plan drawings by Patrick Welsh.

**pp. 66–73: Net-Positive in New England** by Rob Wotzak, FHB issue 267. Photos by Chuck Choi. Floor plan drawings p. 69 by Martha Garstang Hill; drawing p. 73 by Dan Thornton.

**pp. 74–83: Reinventing the Farmhouse** by Rob Whitten, FHB issue 256. Photos by Rob Karosis. Floor plan drawings by Martha Garstang Hill; drawings p. 83 courtesy of Rob Whitten.

**pp. 84–91: Passive House Perfection** by Justin Pauly, FHB issue 235. Photos by Rob Yagid, except p. 85 (top) by Rick Pharaoh. Floor plan drawings p. 87 by Martha Garstang Hill; drawing pp. 90-91 by Don Mannes.

**pp. 92–99: Better Than Average** by Brian Pontolilo, FHB issue 261. Photos by Eric Roth (ericrothphoto.com). Floor plan drawings by Martha Garstang Hill.

**pp. 100–107: Traditional Design, Modern Construction** by Ian McDonald, FHB issue 230. Photos by Rob Yagid, except p. 104, courtesy of Ian McDonald. Drawings pp. 102–103 by Don Mannes; floor plan drawings p. 106 by Martha Garstang Hill

**pp. 108–115: The Architecture of Simplicity** by Brian Pontolilo, FHB issue 259. Photos by John Gruen, except for photo p. 115 courtesy of the Hancock Shaker Village, Pittsfield, Mass. Floor plan drawings by Martha Garstang Hill.

**pp. 116–123: Cold-Climate Collaboration** by Matt O'Malia, FHB issue 243. Photos by Rob Yagid. Floor plan drawings by Martha Garstang Hill.

**pp. 124–131: For the Sake of Simplicity** by Matt Risinger and Eric Rauser, FHB issue 267. Photos by Casey Dunn. Floor plan drawings by Martha Garstang Hill.

**pp. 132–137: Suburban Shift** by Rob Wotzak, FHB issue 275. Photos by Trent Bell. Drawings pp. 134–135 by Don Mannes; floor-plan drawings b. 136 by Patrick Welsh.

**pp. 138–145: Sound Design by Matthew Swett**, FHB issue 275. Photos by Michael Stadler, courtesy of the homeowners Floor plan drawings by Patrick Welsh.

**pp. 146–155: Elevating the Standard of Building** by Sean Groom, FHB issues 260, 267. Photos by Nat Rea, except for p. 151 by Rodney Diaz and p. 153 courtesy of Gladiator. Drawings pp. 148, 150–151 by John Hartman; drawings pp. 152–153 courtesy of SoftPlan.

**pp. 158–163: A Kitchen Built on Tradition** by Rafe Churchill, FHB issue 250. Photos by John Gruen. Floor plan drawing by Martha Garstang Hill.

**pp. 164–167: From Cardboard to Cabinets** by Charles Miller, FHB issue 223. Finished kitchen photos by Charles Miller. Others courtesy of Craig Zehnder. Floor plan drawing by Martha Garstang Hill.

**pp. 168–173: Traditional at First Glance** by Brian Pontolilo, FHB issue 295. Photos by Amanda Kirkpatrick. Floor plan drawing by Patrick Welsh.

The credits for the **Gallery of Farmhouses** appear with the individual farmhouses, beginning on p. 176.